Tightening Noose of Poverty: Abridged

Masood Rezvi

Published By:

LEAD TRUST

(Lucknow Educational And Development Trust)

Flat No. G/C-6, Shahid Apartment, Golagunj, Lucknow (U.P.), India

Email: leadtrust.lko@gmail.com

Website: www.leadtrust.net

1st Abridged Edition: 2016

The royalty earned from this book will be used for charity.

Trust's Vision:

Sustainable global environment for all inhabitants of planet earth.

Trust's Mission:

To generate ideas, spread and diffuse knowledge and inspire and empower humans for inclusive and sustainable developmental environment on the globe.

Trust's Beneficiaries:

All humans without any discrimination.

ISBN-13: 978-1530079186
ISBN-10: 1530079187

DEDICATION

To you – who for reasons whatsoever, became enough aroused to pick
up the book.

And

To all people who crave for an equitable distribution of resources
among all inhabitants of the planet earth.

A MESSAGE FROM ANOTHER PART OF THE PLANET

Hi Masood,

I visited your website – it's a wonderful place that you've built! I was moved by your stories and your plight to help those less fortunate. It is so sad that no matter what country or what city we live, this type of poverty exists. It doesn't seem fair that so many live with so little – that, children have to suffer. You are doing a wonderful thing for these people just by telling their story through your words and your pictures.

You should be very proud of your efforts and I wish you the very best in this endeavour. The people of Lucknow will be a little bit better off because of you.

LIZ

ANOTHER FRIEND WROTE FROM ANOTHER PLACE

I don't know India. I know Kipling – He forces the reader to see through the eyes of the narrator and see the things that are dirty and ugly. And maybe this is why many people hate him as he doesn't apologize for what he presents, but commands attention.

And this you must do for yourself with words as well as with your pictures and you should never apologize for yourself: your insights or your profession.

MARY C LEGG

According to the World Bank, nearly half the world's population—some 2.8 billion people—subsists on $2 a day or less. The number of people living in poverty at the bottom of the wealth pyramid, versus the relative handful at the pyramid's peak, represents what is potentially the most explosive socioeconomic challenge facing the world.

(Emmons, 2007)

CONTENTS

ACKNOWLEDGMENTS

I express my gratitude to the first, only, original and ultimate Creator and Master of the complex system of the universe rather the multiverse, of which me and you and everyone and everything else is only a miniscule but not worthless part – referred by Jews as YHWH, by Hindus as Ishvara, by Christians as God, by Muslims as Allah and by Atheists as the Mother Nature.

My parents, Mr. Syed Shabbir Hasan Rezvi and Mrs. Zakia Begum own the credit for sowing the seeds of this work into the soil of my mind a little more than half a century ago. I don't know in what words should I thank them for this wealth, they passed on to me.

I thank my friend philosopher and guide, the late Mr. Jawed Murtaza, who a little before his sad rather early demise had urged me to publish my thoughts in the form of a book.

I am thankful to Honourable Late Mr. Justice Murtaza Husain for bringing me back into academics, and for always encouraging me for scholarly pursuits.

I also thank Dr. B. N. Singh, Honourable Mr. Justice Imtiyaz Murtaza, Ms. Sameena Imtiyaz, Mr. Aalim Naqvi, Mr. Jamil Akhter, Dr. Anjum Abrar, Mr. Husain Afsar, Mr. Shahid Manzar Abbas Rizvi, Mr. Asghar Mehdi, Ms. Khadija Masood Rizvi, Ms. Samina Javed, Ms. Rubina Jawed Murtaza, Sardar Gurbinder Singh, Dr. Anand Bajpai, Ms. Liz, Ms. Mary C. Legg, Mr. Ashok Mishra, Mr. H. K. Mazhari, Mr. Raihan Azhar Rizvi, Ms. Sumana Zafar, Mr. Murtaza Hasnain Khan, Mr. Nadeem Murtaza, Mr. Fareed Al-Murtaza, Dr. Ali Mahdi Naqvi, Dr. Ehsanul-Haque, Amazon, createspace.com, and their teams for all the encouragement and support without which I could never have attempted to write this book. This list is, of course, incomplete and I sincerely apologise for the same to everyone and anyone whose name I omitted just by human error.

Very special thanks are due to Mr. M. V. Rangacharyulu Faculty at Staff Training College, Punjab National Bank for sparing his valuable time and painstakingly reviewing the manuscript word by word, as well as for his healthy criticism, valuable suggestions and priceless inputs.

I must also thank all those innumerable fellow netizens who showered their encouragements on the social media for the project.

My access to the library of Unity Degree College, Lucknow has been very helpful in garnering the ideas and material for this book. I thank the management, Dr. A. B. Siddiqui, the Principal and Ms. Afeefa Zaidi and Ms. Rabab Ara, the Librarians for their cooperation.

I also thank all my students, especially those who have attended my macroeconomics lectures, because their questions and queries have opened to me ever new realities regarding the working of macroeconomic variables in our economy.

I must also thank the Government of Uttar Pradesh for nominating me as a member of the State Level Committee for Implementation of the Prime Minister's New 15 Point Programme for the Welfare of Minorities, which gave me some more insight into the working of development programmes of our government.

Masood Rezvi

Lucknow,
November 20, 2015

PREFACE

S o you have picked up the book and are reading it.

But why?

Perhaps the title or the picture on the cover page attracted you.

But why?

Were you pained? Was it too sickening? Did it remind you of something familiar? Or, was it something quite unfamiliar?

Maybe it is a story of your own land and your own neighbourhood. Or, maybe for you it is a story of those far off nations where morons sub-humans inefficient lazy and lethargic non-intelligent people live, who are simply losing the battle of survival in the struggle for existence and will inevitably be wiped off the face of the planet in the process of further speciation of the present day human species *Homo sapiens*. Who are just as much worthy of care as is any other species of primates like the chimpanzees or gorillas – and deserve nothing more!

Whatever the reason, let me tell you at the very onset that this book does not attempt to satisfy any of your questions or queries or bolster any of your beliefs. At the end, you will perhaps be more perplexed and confused and more directionless than you are now at the beginning. Your itch will only increase. So please leaf through further at your own risk and responsibility.

Let me also tell you, it is not a technical book. It does not treat the subject according to any recognised discipline of study, anthropology, sociology or economics or whatsoever. It is intended for anyone and everyone who gets enough aroused to touch it. The book is meant for and dedicated to that person alone.

The language used is Indian English. The system of spellings used is British, except in quotes from American authors. I have tried to explain all Indian jargons and acronyms in the glossary for the non-Indian readers and hope they will not become an impediment in smooth reading for anyone.

1 PROLOGUE

> *The Child is father of the man;*
>
> *And I could wish my days to be*
>
> *Bound each to each by natural piety.*
>
> (Wordsworth)

I suppose there are people who grew from a child into a man or a woman.

I didn't.

I am still the child I was. I will always be the child that I am. I never want to grow into anything which is not that child.

My earliest memories take me back to cosy sweet dreams of Kolkata, in my bed at the side of *Nani Amma* my maternal granny, she reading out stories of fairies and princes, good and gallant people who ventured into unknown territories and always helped those who were helpless.

I am that prince who is so helpful for everyone. I thought.

My granny was one of the daughters of the famous Urdu scholar of Hyderabad – Allama Ali Haider Nazm Tabatabai who was the first to translate the famous English poem "Elegy Written in a Country Churchyard" by Thomas Gray into his Urdu poem "gor-e-ghariban", and the first to write explanation of the Urdu *Diwan* of Mirza Ghalib.

My maternal grandfather Hakeem Sadiq became so famous in his practice of *Unani* medicine that King George VI bestowed upon him the prestigious title of *Shifa-ul-Mulk* (Cure for the Nation). He died much before the marriage of my parents and was survived there at Kolkata by his sons, one of them a *hakeem* and the other an allopath. Both had their clinics on the ground floor of the same house in which they lived.

I remember sneaking down into their clinic watching intently seeing them their patients. The pain on the faces of their patients and the hope of relief that twinkled in their eyes always aroused in my heart a deep sense of sympathy for them and a great sense of pride about the medical profession. I would go into the dispensary and watch the Bengali compounder *babu* prepare mixtures so efficiently. I was aware how much my uncles were of use and importance to those humans who came to them seeking mitigation of their maladies.

I will be a doctor like my uncles, how noble it was. I decided.

My father Syed Shabbir Hasan Rezvi was a lecturer in the department of Urdu and Persian at RDS College Muzaffarpur. I was his only son, the fruit of a very late marriage. He was a gold medalist and record setter at Patna University in his postgraduate examination in Persian.

I have to be a gold-medalist like my father. I used to think.

My parents wanted me to learn to live on my own. They did not want me to become like those children who were very much dependent on their parents for everything, but they could not afford to send me to a good boarding school somewhere. I was thus, taken by my sister (My only sister) to Darbhanga. Her husband, Prof. Murtaza Azhar Rizvi, was a lecturer of philosophy (Ultimately he Became Professor of Philosophy) at Darbhanga. He was a very lively, jolly and strong man. He was rather crazy about helping people. I remember him sitting many nights at a stretch at the bedside of ailing distant relations, putting his own comfort in jeopardy for their comfort. He was a titan in his subject and I remember how deeply he was admired by those who were around him. In many aspects, he became my role model. He always advocated a scientific way of thinking.

I will be a researcher. My dream took a further refinement.

Two more of his passions I imbibed – he was a voracious reader and he was a keen photographer. I also love reading almost anything from any school of thought without any prejudice and I love shooting just any scene that catches my eyes and love sharing the excitement of that beauty with the world.

My father retired from his job the year I completed my High School and that brought a drastic reduction in the family financial resources. After completing my Intermediate, I appeared for joint competitive examination for admission to medical colleges as also a competitive examination for admission to B.Sc. Agriculture at Rajendra Agricultural University Pusa, Samastipur Bihar.

I could not make through the test for Medical Studies but was selected for admission into the B.Sc. Agriculture curriculum. In my class, there were many who took second and third attempts for admission in medicine and many of them got through. I remember remaining awake one night and thinking the implication of a second attempt at seeking admission in medicine. My parents had grown old. I did not have a brother to take care of them. I did not, therefore, have time to waste. I had done quite well in the first trimester and my seniors were getting jobs quickly on completing the course. I thus decided to remain in the stream I was. Slowly I inculcated a pride of studying a subject which was a weapon of technology in the human fight against hunger. I started enjoying plant breeding and genetics especially, took the examination for the award of Junior Research Fellowship of Indian Council of Agricultural Research in plant breeding and was selected. That was a great day for me. I was no more dependent financially on anyone for my studies. I took admission into M.Sc. Agriculture in plant breeding.

I must mention that I had the honour of having Dr. B. N. Singh as my research guide in M.Sc. Dr. Singh later worked as Director, Central Rice Research Institute Cuttack and Director Research at Birsa Agricultural University, Ranchi, Jharkhand, and is now through his not for profit organisation Centre for Research and Development at Gorakhpur busy in breeding rice varieties of high value and popularising them among the farmers with a missionary zeal. I was and still am one of his pet students. He is another role model for me. Under Dr. Singh, I worked on genotype-environment interaction in semi-dwarf varieties of rice for my M.Sc. thesis. Dr. Singh was also the professor-in-charge for seminars. Postgraduate students were required to give a seminar which was rated for one-course credit. For my seminar, I chose a subject which in those days was quite new (Transposable Genetic Elements – Transposons

– or the Jumping Genes. In fact Barbara McClintock had won Nobel Prize for this discovery in that year i.e., 1983 only). Never, in life can I forget the shining in Dr. Singh's eyes when that seminar proved to be a great success.

I completed my M.Sc. and got a job as agriculture officer at area office of New Bank of India at Agra almost simultaneously.

I was also able to fulfil one more of my cherished dreams at this stage – *Like my father I won the University Gold Medal.*

At Agra, I enjoyed coordinating lending for agriculture and other priority sectors by our branches in Agra, Etah, Etawah, Mainpuri, Aligarh and Firozabad districts, and at many times worked on deputation at rural branches for processing of loan applications of farm folk.

I mingled with them extensively and always loved their honest and simple ways. I had a missionary euphoria. I was also given the responsibility of coordinating with the district authorities and I attended all meetings from Block Level Bankers Committee Meetings to District Level Review Committee Meetings. The farm credit and credit to weaker sectors increased phenomenally and a later study by the Project Monitoring and Evaluation Cell of the bank praised the good utilization of loan for the actual economic upliftment of the beneficiaries.

A few years later I was taken to the Regional Office Lucknow by our Deputy General Manager, especially to help clear a big backlog of returns and statements that had become pending from that office. I achieved that goal within three months. It was actually only a problem of identifying the reason for the default. This was so simple that branches were not getting the necessary proforma every time when they were required to submit the information. I along with my two other colleagues and batch mates, Mr. Mishra and Mr. Ranga started the practice of sending the complete set of formats every month to each branch. In addition, I used to attend Meetings of State Level Bankers Committee too along with the Deputy General Manager and coordinated with agencies like National Bank for Agriculture and Rural Development (NABARD).

During my stay at Lucknow, I did System Development Skills Course in Computers from NIIT and was again the highest scorer in my batch.

After the merger of New Bank of India with Punjab National Bank I was transferred to Partawal Branch at Maharajganj District in Eastern Uttar Pradesh. I was required to look after all branches in Maharajganj District. I was transferred after a while to the Gorakhpur regional office and was posted as an officer in Planning and Development Cell. My duties included monitoring deposit and advances growth and profitability, maintaining idle cash balance at a minimum possible level in the region, arranging cash diversion orders from the RBI and ensuring timely flow of information to the zonal office.

It was during this time that the first PC was provided to Gorakhpur regional office. No specific package was till then available and the software provided with the PC consisted of d-Base, Lotus and WordStar. Keeping in view my computer training, the system was given in my charge and very quickly I not only converted all analysis of my section in d-base programs written by myself but also helped other sections do the same. The zonal office recognised my achievements and I was often deputed to other regional offices to motivate and train them in using the machine.

Another challenge that came in was the desire of the management to get ISO 9002 certification for the regional offices. The task was assigned to me at regional office Gorakhpur. I prepared all the documents, trained the staff; and Gorakhpur became the first regional office in the zone to get that certification. I was promoted and posted at the zonal office Lucknow. I was given the duty of managing non-performing assets (NPA) of the zone and, in addition, was required to associate deeply with the ISO certification process of other regional offices and of the zonal office itself. I was required to train staff in the staff training college as guest faculty in the field of use of computers, quality system, non-performing asset management, compromise policy etc. I must proudly mention that I was brought to zonal office by, and worked under Mr. U. S. Bhargava the then Deputy General Manager who is always remembered, as the man who gave new vision to banking in Punjab National Bank in Uttar Pradesh and who won the title of *Uttar Pradesh Ratna* from the All India Conference of Intellectuals. The title was delivered to him by the Honourable Governor of U.P. in 1998.

I revere Mr. Bhargava as my teacher in many areas of Management.

In the year 2000, the Management came with a voluntary retirement scheme. It flashed to me, though I was doing well in my job, that I needed more freedom to make my own experimentations, more space to let the child that I was play freely. I opted for it. I was the youngest officer in the zone to go for voluntary retirement under the scheme.

Since then I am freelancing in many areas in Lucknow and now *I just want to spread my wings and fulfil the remaining dreams of the child I am.*

I am looking forward to the opportunity to work for the downtrodden – opportunity, to do things for them. I know them I have seen them so closely – The glass industry workers of Firozabad, the leather and cardboard workers of Agra, the carpet workers of Bhadohi, the small marginal farmers the agricultural labour, the *Dalits* typically living on the southern flank of every village. Women – always treated as second sex in almost every society.

Lately, when I started roaming around in the city with my camera I realised that this is not one city; it actually consists of two cities living in the same space. One which consists of us which at its lowest stratum perhaps has the urban domestic workers and manual masonry labourers, and the other and quite different – the dwellers of cardboard and plastic sheet huts, who live on picking our garbage! I wonder, does our society think of them as humans – of members of the same species? Have we ever thought of them?

This book is a collection of different write-ups rendered on paper at different times and is meant for anyone who shares my passions.

Don't you???

Picture 1: This is not a refugee camp! It is peacetime –
Another fine morning for city dwellers like me and you. A
small child and her mother are seen in their
neighbourhood of houses – yes *HOUSES* – built of used
cardboard boxes and thrown away plastic sheets in
Lucknow, the capital of Uttar Pradesh, in India. In the
background the historical clock tower of Lucknow can be
seen. Who is responsible? In a democracy, we the people!
(*Photo: Masood Rezvi*)

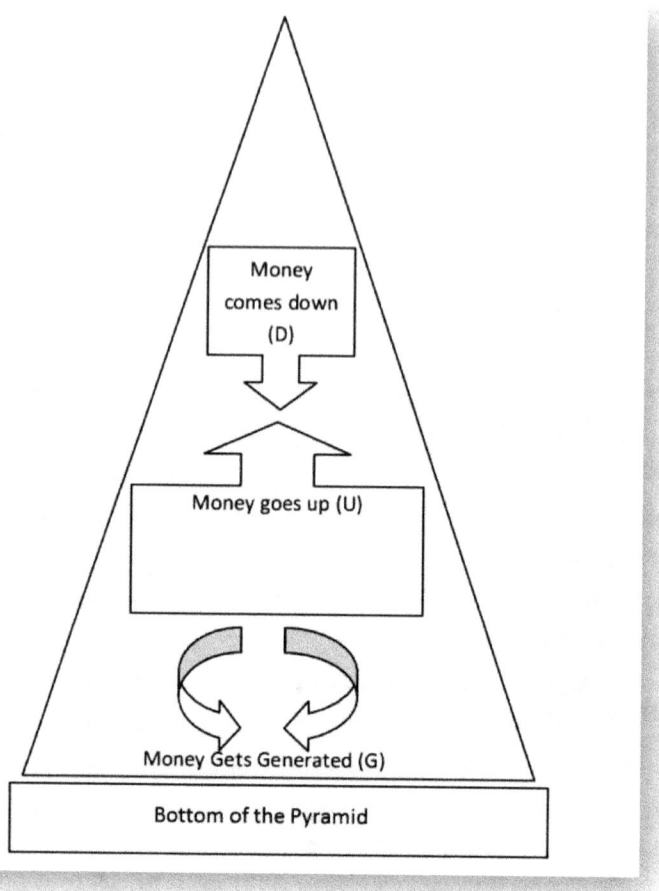

Illustration 1: Pyramid Visualised. (*Illustration: Masood Rezvi*)

2 LIFT THE BOTTOM. CAN YOU?

It is a great and welcome change that the corporate sector is becoming aware of the fact that for doing a good business nearly half of the world population which lives on an income of less than $2 a day cannot be ignored.

Scholars at high-class places of learning and investigation like the Harvard Business School are taking a serious interest in the matter. As members of the School's Global Poverty Project (GPP), Kash Rangan, John Quelch, and other faculty members have studied and researched the issue of business and global poverty for quite some time. They believe that in pursuing its own self-interest in the opening and expanding the bottom of pyramid market, a business can make a profit while serving the poorest of consumers and contributing to development. As Rangan explains, "For business, the bulk of emerging markets worldwide is at the bottom of the pyramid so it makes good business sense—not a sense of do-gooding—to go after it." (Emmons, 2007). I think it can be hoped that one day they will be able to make at least a majority of prudent entrepreneurs and capitalists think and believe in what Rangan has said.

Perhaps some day businesses will know that the bottom of the wealth and income pyramid has to be taken care of, not for do-gooding but for the long term maximisation of their own profits. But I am sure it will be really a tough task for anyone to come up with a formula, through which, those at the top make money, and those at the bottom also make money.

I can very well at least hypothetically visualize it. This can be achieved only by speeding up the circulation of money from top to bottom and then back to the top. But since the concern for profit maximisation without a sense of do-gooding, will compel the businesses to ensure that the money they get back is more than what they sent down, duly compensated for the time value of money; it will be necessary to ensure that the money percolates to the lowest level of the bottom and there it is gainfully employed so as to multiply many, many times.

Only then part of the money so generated will be able to sublimate to the top after a part of it is left back at the bottom, at least enough to increase the future purchasing power there, and to strengthen their role as a demand generator in future.

One of the problems with economics and other social sciences as against physical and biological sciences is that the content of these subjects is the behaviour of humans themselves. Thus, every group involved in the study, views any particular result or implementation of a solution as for or against its own short-term benefits, in the backdrop of its own vested interests in the issue.

Will we, then, be able to develop a model in which the top and the bottom of the pyramid are equally benefited in the short term? By common sense, it appears that the pyramid has taken its typical pyramid shape only because money has historically and traditionally moved against gravity gradient – from bottom to top.

The top naturally will not want money to move in the opposite direction!

So the only solution possible is to lift the pyramid from the base to a place where the bottom too is, at least, high enough to eat and live with basic amenities and is able to provide an opportunity for individuals at the bottom, to move upwards, if they strive for it.

But how low is the *bottom* of the pyramid? *How low*?

Illustration 1 makes it amply clear that without do-gooding an investment in the 'market' at the bottom of pyramid will help in improving the living condition of the people at the bottom only if money generated (G) is greater than the money which goes up (U), which in turn is greater than the money which comes down (D).

Even if it so happens, the money left behind (L=G-U), perhaps will be so less in comparison to the money that moves up (U), that when divided by the large number of consumers at the bottom, it will make the gap between each such consumer and the rich investor at the top of the pyramid much more pronounced and wider, than before.

Thus, I feel it is very difficult to agree with Rangan, that without a sense of do-gooding his scheme will ever succeed in helping the poor at the bottom of the pyramid albeit it may help those at the top in making some more profit from this 'bulk of the market' segment.

Before we move on to the next chapter, let us pause for a moment and also try to contemplate what could be the possible different motives which may emerge from Rangan's suggestion for the top of the pyramid to go after the bottom. The three possible motives that emerge are:

1. *A sense of do-gooding and not a good business sense*: This is what the saints and ascetics have been preaching and practicing since long. Those who have this motive basically deny themselves the worldly pleasures and are even ready to harm themselves in order to help the less fortunate fellow creatures. This view has been bitterly criticised on the basis of inefficiency that it supposedly produces in the society. It is argued that those who do not produce anything are encouraged and rewarded by this system to remain unproductive. Because they take it for granted that those who produce are duty bound to feed them and take care of their needs and thus they do not have any necessity to take the risk of an enterprise or toil of hard labour. Those who produce, on the other hand, waste a large chunk of their resources – capital as well as time and energy on feeding these *parasites* while the same could very well have been harnessed for further production opportunities. However, under this situation a person at the top waters down the bottom of the pyramid, howsoever unproductive it might be, with full awareness that what he or she is sending down to the bottom will rather never come back to him or her in this life, and thus the gap

narrows down automatically and the pyramid might start taking a somewhat trapezoidal shape or may tend to become rectangular in shape. Religions, almost all, rather all, without an exception, have therefore promoted the concept of life after life where do-gooding will be rewarded, by the beneficent God, and the reverse will be punished.

2. *Good business sense tempered with a sense of do-gooding*: What is a good business sense? Well, consult any standard textbook on financial management. My favourite is Prof. Prasanna Chandra's book (Chandra, 1979), but you can consult any other standard text. Most probably you will find that the very first or second chapter of the book is dedicated to the objective of financial management. You will find that all authorities on the subject these days agree that the objective of the financial management should be wealth maximisation of shareholders. Please do not confuse it with profit earning or even with profit maximisation. The two are quite different. If you are eager to know how they are different, please refer a book on financial management. Many of the authors are quite candid and honest in telling us that during the course of a business, there may arise, situations where the manager is to choose between the objective of wealth maximisation and other objectives like quality assurance, employee welfare, customer satisfaction, etc. In all such conditions until and unless compelled by the law of the land to do otherwise, he or she should select wealth maximisation as the goal to be pursued, and sacrifice the other goals. This is a good business sense defined. And this is the gospel which our b-schools are busy preaching, the world over. We may still, however, presume that there might be some businesses who do not endorse to the technical wisdom preached by the savants of business management, or may be, are a little irrational due to their childhood upbringing or personal memories; and mix do-gooding with a good business sense, or are compelled by a

government genuinely concerned about its citizens at the bottom of pyramid to do so. In such a case also, some of the money percolating down to the bottom of the pyramid will not go up again, and to some extent will be able to lift the bottom at least above the basic subsistence level.

3. *Good business sense and not a sense of do-gooding*: This is the motive advocated by Rangan. It basically is a bizarre representation of a mind which looks upon the world as a market, and not as a home. And has discovered that the bulk of it lies at the bottom on which the corporate world should swoop down with a good business sense and not a sense of do-gooding. With the managers in the corporate world chasing the objective of wealth maximisation, how will it help in lifting the bottom up, can be anybody's guess.

Sorry dear, for me there is a difference between home and market and this planet is my home and your home too; please don't make it a market. In a home, you feed your baby though it is still unproductive. You do not kill your terminally sick spouse though he or she is not productive. You, still in most of the civilised societies provide for your old and ailing parents though they are not productive anymore, you even care for your pet cat which does not help you increase your wealth in any way. But, in a market, you do not do these things. If you convert your home into a market it will be doomed to eternal destruction.

So please remember that planet earth is our home. Let us not convert it into a pure market.

Further, it is not true that those at the bottom of the pyramid are intrinsically not productive. They are humans. They belong to the same species, I and you belong to. They are potentially as productive as you and me. A systematic care, upliftment, and empowerment programme for them may give the world its most brilliant scientists, artists, doctors and entrepreneurs from among these people.

A sense of do-gooding is, therefore, indispensable!

> *While the proportion of the people living below poverty line has been declining over the years, the rate of such decline has been quite low, except during the recent past. Nearly 80 percent of the people living below poverty line are located in rural areas, with a large share coming from the category of wage workers.*
>
> (Ministry of Rural Development GoI, 2012-2013)

3 WHO IS POOR WHO NOT? THE CONUNDRUM OF THE POVERTY LINE

omeone said, don't remember who, that there are three categories of a lie; lie blatant lie and statistics. You may or may not agree with this statement but I feel deeply inclined to agree with the fact that statistics published by governments and government aided and sponsored projects of economic surveys, serve little purpose other than producing an imbroglio of numbers and definitions which rather keep you away and distracted from the core of the problem under study. A good work of snow jobbing! (Lewicki, Saunders, & Barry, 2008).

It is very much akin to a recent joke I read on Facebook: If you don't read newspapers you are uninformed; if you do, you are misinformed.

I understand that the UN thinks that those who earn less than $1.25 a day are poor. As discussed in the foregoing chapter Rangan et al, think that bottom of the pyramid is at $2 a day. While the committees and subcommittees of highly paid scholars who themselves earn and spend thousands of rupees a day have come out with some beautiful definitions moving the poverty line up and down, down and down. Great game! Let's see:

1. Tendulkar Committee which submitted its report to the government in November 2009 estimated the new all India poverty line for the year 2004-05 for rural areas at ₹446.68 per capita per month and for urban areas at ₹578.86 per capita per month (₹1.00= $0.015443, today i.e. on Oct 12, 2015). Thus according to this report a person living in rural India was poor if he earned less than

$(446.68 \div 30) \times 0.015443 = \$0.229936$ in a 30 day month, or even less in 31 day months; and a person living in urban India was poor if he earned less than $(578.86 \div 30) \times 0.015443 = \$0.297978$ or even less in 31 day months! Great! Forget about \$2. People earning that much are super rich in India! Anyhow, by that standard 41.8 percent of the rural population and 25.7 percent of the urban population was below the poverty line in 2004-05. For the country as a whole people below the poverty line were estimated to be 37.2 percent.

2. On July 22, 2013, the Planning Commission released poverty estimates for the year 2011-12. The poverty line was fixed at ₹27.20 per capita per day for rural areas and at ₹33.33 per capita per day for urban areas. This translates to \$0.420050 for rural areas and \$0.514715 for urban areas, per person per day at the prevalent conversion rate today! As per this standard, it was reported for the country as a whole that *only* 21.9 percent of the population lived below the poverty line in 2011-12 (25.7 percent in rural areas and 13.7 percent in urban areas).

Hurray! Lo! In five or so years how much poverty was reduced!!

3. Rangarajan Committee after re-examining the issue of poverty(line) submitted its report to the government in June 2014. It (re)defined the poverty line in 2011-12 at ₹47.00 (\$0.725821) per capita per day for urban areas and ₹32.00 (\$0.494176) per capita per day in rural areas and estimated that according to this definition 29.5% of Indians as a whole lived below poverty line (30.9 percent in rural areas and 26.4 percent in urban areas) in the year 2011-12.

Are you not yet thoroughly impressed with the great statistical talent that we do have in our country? You have already seen that our government claims that *"While the proportion of the people living below poverty line has been declining over the years, the rate of such decline has been quite low, except during the recent past."*

An impressive achievement of the recent past!

Isn't it?

Anyhow, I hope by now you must be having a profound understanding of who is poor and who not in India. If you still don't understand it well, don't move ahead. Re-read this chapter then read it again and then re-read it till you understand!

The source of the information: (Puri & Misra, 2015).

Every night on the outskirts of Manila, thousands of people lie down to sleep amid acres of rotting food and industrial detritus in a vast urban dumping ground called Payatas. At dawn, they rise and swarm across a featureless landscape of trash and filth, hunting for scraps of anything they can eat or sell. Payatas and the orderly, verdant Harvard Business School campus—nearly equals, as it happens, in terms of the acreage they occupy—are separated by a gulf far greater than any measure of miles or statistics.

(Emmons, 2007)

4 A TALE OF TWO CITIES

If you live in Lucknow or any other Indian city like Mumbi, Kolkata or Delhi, you only need to have open eyes and a discerning mind to notice that this is not one city. The city is actually split into two distinct parts, completely alien to each other. One, which comprises of people like me and you; and the other, consisting of people who live in 'colonies', built from thrown away cardboard boxes and plastic sheets, or simply anywhere at the roadside. They do not have any job or profession, not even the most menial ones, except, for example picking up trash to sell recyclable items to *kabadiwallahs*, the sellers of recyclable paper and containers, etc.

Their names are not included in the voter lists; they have no identity documents and have no ration cards. In fact, I am sure they are not included in the census and do not count in the population below poverty line reckoned by our government, planners, and the statisticians. They share their ecosystem with the ubiquitous stray street dogs, bulls, cows and calves.

Is this the bulk of emerging markets which according to Rangan et al; makes good business sense—not a sense of do-gooding—to go after it?

Market or no market, good business sense or no business sense, they are humans; biologically and genetically they are members of the same species of primates the *Homo sapiens* to which I and you also belong. They are Indian citizens as much as any other citizen and the Indian Constitution guarantees to them equal rights, nay special protection. Article 39 of The Directive Principles of State Policy clearly states that the *State shall, in particular, direct its policy towards securing—*

(a) that the citizens, men and women equally, have the right to an adequate means of livelihood; (b) that the ownership and control of the material resources of the community are so distributed as best to subserve the common good; (c) that the operation of the economic system does not result in the concentration of wealth and means of production to the common detriment; (d) that there is equal pay for equal work for both men and women; (e) that the health and strength of workers, men and women, and the tender age of children are not abused and that citizens are not forced by economic necessity to enter vocations unsuited to their age or strength; (f) that children are given opportunities and facilities to develop in a healthy manner and in conditions of freedom and dignity and that childhood and youth are protected against exploitation and against moral and material abandonment.

Who is responsible for the present state of affairs then?

Who could be, except the ultimate sovereign!

Who is the ultimate sovereign in a democracy?

Who else could be, but "We the People"!

Yes, we the people, me and you – by using our voting rights unwisely on the basis of trivial and unimportant issues or by abstaining from using it, have created this misery and are directly responsible for it.

But why we?

Only we are responsible because there has neither been a war which displaced them, nor a famine, nor any other natural calamity, which could have pushed these people to such an abysmal position.

Where do they originate?

If it was a fixed number of originally marginalised people due to circumstances beyond our control their numbers would have eventually declined, by many climbing up the socioeconomic ladder, with the help of the government and non-government charity organisations, a plethora of which is registered and supposedly working in our country fighting poverty.

Not relying on any census or even sample survey estimating the change in their population – because neither have I been able to lay my hands on any such data nor do I believe in the correctness or authenticity of such statistics – on the strength of my own gut feeling I claim that the number has never declined. It is rather increasing. I will love if agencies jump in to prove me wrong and collect and compile reliable statistics for this purpose.

Where do they come from then?

If you want a reality check, come along with me for a morning walk on the Hardoi Road between *Ghas Mandi* and *Dubagga.* These are the manual labour markets in the city. You will find hundreds of men women and even minor children, gathered at each junction of the roads waiting to be hired for masonry work by construction contractors or private people for some physical work which may more often than not be also hazardous for a daily wage of $2 or a little more.

Only some of them are lucky enough to find someone ready to hire them. Others go on waiting and waiting for many days, often not having enough money to eat even once in a day. They generally come to the city from neighbouring rural and semi-urban areas in the hope of making some money. They come because they have lost the traditional source of earning – their farmland – slowly and slowly to moneylenders, to builders, to government projects; or even to banking institutions because the funds made available to them were not enough or in time to produce enough return for them to pay back their debt and interest thereupon. Frustrated, some of them return to their native places to become bonded labourers of big landlords, while others soon become sick, meet with some accident etc and become incapacitated for hard labour.

This source feeds the cloud of the group under discussion as the primary source or the root stock. The women and even minor girls breed in this hostile environment, not only in a family arrangement of some sort but also as a result of sexual exploitation by *kabadiwallahs,* truck and bus drivers, etc who during their long journeys prefer to park their vehicles for a rest near such ghettos. Look at Picture 1 again. You will notice many big vehicles parked in the background.

Thus, to my mind this pathetic situation is the direct result of following *man made* felonies:

1. Looking upon the globe as a 'market' with 'good business sense' and not as a home shared with other inhabitants with a sense of 'do-gooding'.

2. Exploitation of farmers driving them out of their farmlands.

3. Sexual exploitation of women and children.

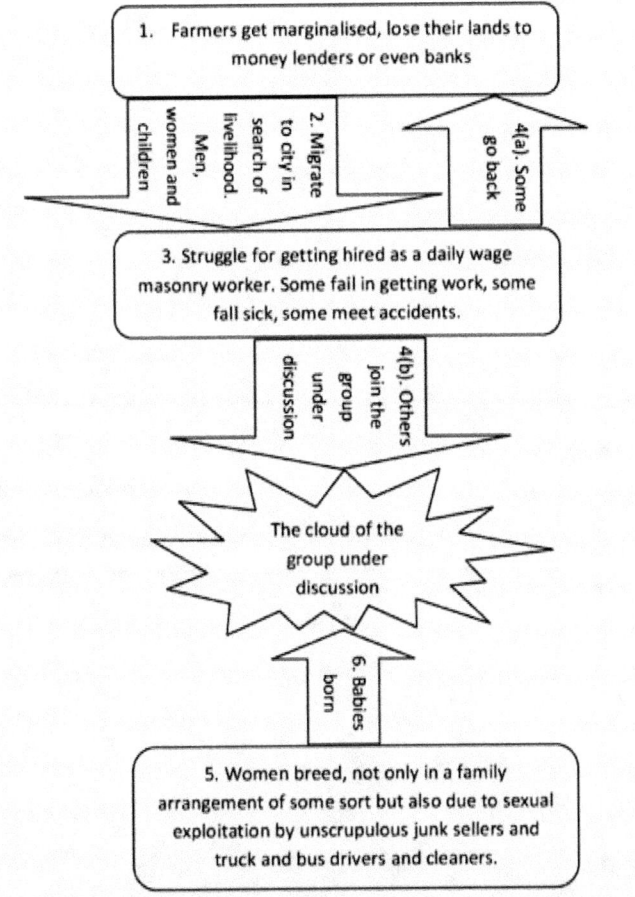

Illustration 2: Where do they come from? (Illustration: Masood Rezvi)

> *Agreed this video is unbelievably heart crushing.*
>
> (Deepika Ramesh –
>
> A commentator on my video at YouTube)

5 BUY PENS AT BEIRUT AND EAT FILTH AT LUCKNOW

One fine morning I came across the following post by a senior journalist friend in a WhatsApp group:–

An unknown person was selling pens in the streets of Beirut. His daughter Reem was sleeping on his shoulder. Wrinkles of anxiety were clearly seen on the face of this refugee and someone photographed him.

Gissur Simonarson, a social worker from Oslo twitted this picture which reached his six thousand strong followers. He had commented on the picture: *This is an extremely touching picture. Look at the face of this man. Look at the way he is holding the pens. It seems that these pens are all which he possesses in this world.*

Within hours, people around the world lined up to help that poor unknown fellow. But social worker Gissur was unaware of this man's name, and of in which part of Beirut the picture was taken. Social media activists joined hands in a campaign for searching him through hashtag #BuyPens. Within two days he was traced. When this fellow Abdul, a father of two children knew that entire world was searching him he was extremely delighted. Abdul had fled his hometown in Syria and landed in Beirut as a refugee. Before the war broke in, in Syria, Abdul used to work at a chocolate factory. He is one of the 40,00,000 registered refugees, who are struggling for their lives in Turkey, Lebanon and Jordan. Gissur made a page spearheading a campaign for collecting $5,000, and the target was achieved within thirty minutes and within 24 hours people donated more than $80,000 for Abdul! When Abdul came to know of it, he broke into tears and said he would now be able to send his children to school. I verified the story on Google and it is true.

(Kassem & Jamieson, 2015). A great job, indeed! Proving that humanity is alive and people still get motivated to do things purely with a sense of do-gooding.

This, however instantly reminded me of the video that I had uploaded, under screen name *folkographer* on YouTube in 2008 (https://youtu.be/wkh_CLhORvg). The video shows slum children chewing thrown away sugarcane stubs from a heap of filth here at Lucknow. The post has attracted 46K + views so far. And all sort of comments - many of them from those who were moved to tears about the plight of the children and were concerned about doing something to help them, but some which uncover a heap of filth human minds may contain which is dirtier than the filth from which these children are eating (It may be interesting for you to go to the URL and read all those comments).

These children are not a stray case. There are hundreds and thousands like them in Lucknow alone. Such abject poverty is found not only here, but also in many other parts of our planet. Let me quote Emmons once again even at the cost of repetition: *Every night on the outskirts of Manila, thousands of people lie down to sleep amid acres of rotting food and industrial detritus in a vast urban dumping ground called Payatas. At dawn, they rise and swarm across a featureless landscape of trash and filth, hunting for scraps of anything they can eat or sell. Payatas and the orderly, verdant Harvard Business School campus—nearly equals, as it happens, in terms of the acreage they occupy—are separated by a gulf far greater than any measure of miles or statistics.* (Emmons, 2007).

If you watch the video and then look at Abdul's pictures you will for sure know that these children are living a life, much, much more miserable than that Abdul was living or his likes are living in Beirut or other places.

Abdul is a refugee. Armed conflict, an apparent and dramatic cause of human misery is the cause of his pains. But these children are not refugees. There was no war around. Who has pushed them to this stage then?

We! All of us who are happy with the wealth maximisation based system that rules our world.

Let's burn with passion for a change. No amount of charity will help ameliorate the situation only a change in the way we think and act can. Only a do-gooding oriented thinking can.

If outstanding debt increases by ₹1000 then the odds that the household is one with a suicide victim increases by 6 per cent ...

(Mishra, 2007)

6 FARMERS AND DEBT TRAP

The Hand Book of Agriculture published by the Indian Council of Agricultural Research records that "*Various studies conducted at different times on rural indebtedness revealed that the farming community was in the clutches of local money lenders. The terms of lending by these moneylenders were unfavourable and inimical to the interests of the farmers.*" (Indian Council of Agricultural Research, 1987).

What actually was unfavourable and inimical to the interests of farmers? A little introspection will reveal that this was two-fold:

1) The provision of credit to farmers, especially to poor small and marginal farmers and the interest rate on such credit, was entirely dependent on the sweet will of the moneylender (mainly local *Banias* i.e., traders and goldsmiths) on whom they depended exclusively for their liquidity.

2) The moneylender was powerful both in terms of his knowledge and access to the prevalent legal system and in terms of muscle power and his ability to intimidate the borrower as and when he so wished.

These studies coupled with the realisation that hunger if allowed to perpetuate in the masses, could pave ways for revolutions which may even be a violent upheaval, forced different governments in the past to formulate different measures to check the local moneylender and to make available institutional finance to farmers. The biggest move in this direction was the nationalisation of banks, pushing them systematically to open branches in rural areas; as also fixation of targets for lending for direct agriculture and other identified priority sectors of the economy like small scale industries etc.

Governments also stepped in through introduction of subsidy based schemes for the weaker sector like IRDP, SCP, DWCRA, SEUUP, SEPUP, SEEUY, and PMRY etc. It is no secret that though the debtor on paper was the farmer and the weaker sector borrower, a good chunk of subsidy leaked to other people.

There is no denying of the fact that agricultural lending was finally taken up by the banks and the local moneylender was eventually replaced by the institutional moneylender (the banks) in a big way.

At the national level, the total direct finance of scheduled commercial banks to agriculture grew from 235 crore rupees (1crore=10 million) in 1970-71 to 95565 crore rupees in 2004-05 (406.66 times!). The total indirect finance (indirect finance to agriculture is lending for fertilizer distribution, and loans to electricity boards for energisation of pump sets, loans to farmers through agriculture credit societies etc,) similarly grew from 143 crore rupees in 1970-71 to 36071 crore rupees in 2004-05 (252.25 times). The total direct plus indirect finance to agriculture by the scheduled commercial banks grew from 378 crore rupees in 1970-71 to 131636 crore rupees in 2004-05 (348.24 times) - (Reserve Bank of India, 2005-06)

In the same time period i.e., 1970-71 to 2004-05 the national food grain production improved from 99.50 million tonnes to 198.36 million tonnes (The growth was 1.99 times only!!) – Source of statistics is the same as above. Well, let me add that I could not find figures in terms of rupees instead of million tonnes, for production (had it been there it would have been easier to compare it with the growth in institutional credit).

But what is available is sufficient for us to question why the replacement of local moneylender by the institutional moneylender did not result in an increase in food grain production to the tune of even one hundredth of the increase in money lent by the institutional moneylender, to the agricultural sector?

I could not find any statistics on the total indebtedness of the farmer (debts owed to local money lender + debts owed to institutional money lender) then and now. I suppose and hypothesize that if we add up the two, the total debt of the farming community has increased to a much higher level during this time period, without any significant increase in their production, and income.

No doubt, there have been many studies and attempts to improve the flow of institutional credit to the farming sector and the weaker sectors of the societies. Issues of undue delay in disposal of loan applications, the untimely release of funds, the inaccurate amount of finance etc have been discussed many times over. A recent attempt in this direction is the "Report of the Working Group to Examine the Procedures and Processes of Agricultural Loans" (Swarnkar, 2007). The Group, headed by Mr. C. P. Swarnkar, has elaborated many points and has made a recommendation for correct and proper maintenance of Loan Application Receipt and Disposal Register etc, of dispensing with the need of No Dues Certificates from different banks on computerisation of land records and other such things.

While giving recommendations for State Governments the Group has inter-alia recorded the following:

"Recovery Procedures

3.22 Of late, the farmers in many areas have been susceptible to propaganda against repayment of their dues. This, in turn, discourages the banks to lend in such areas where repayment record is bad. Simplified procedures and quick repayment of loans are two sides of the same coin. Simplified procedures not only encourage farmers to take loans but also encourage them to repay. On the other hand, if the repayment record is good, the bankers would be encouraged to adopt simplified procedure. Proper counselling and financial education can help the farmers to see through this and understand the nuances. Support from the State Governments in the recovery efforts of the banks will also encourage them to lend more aggressively. The Group recommends that SLBCs in the respective states may bring this fact to the notice of the State Governments and coordinate with them in this regard."

On the other hand, the Group has made no recommendation for the banks to evolve a foolproof system to ensure that State Recovery Acts (UP Agricultural Credit Act and UP Public Money Recovery of Dues Act – in Uttar Pradesh, for example) are not misused and abused. No system of pre RC-filing scrutiny and post RC-filing audit and inspection has been recommended.

Let me elaborate. The entire story progresses in this way –

1) The farmer was in the grip of local village *Bania* moneylender, who exploited him because he, the moneylender, was more resourceful than the borrower.

2) Banks were nationalised and took over the farm credit almost completely.

3) They were subsequently privatised and their shares were taken up by moneyed people all over.

4) They are any day much more resourceful and organised than the local moneylender was! There is a hype about freeing of the farmer from the clutches of the moneylender but isn't it so that actually, the moneylender has grown more organised and powerful through just becoming a shareholder of the banks, and can even tell the governments that it needs special coercive and unilateral recovery powers from the Government for recovery from the poor people?

Unfortunately, I could not find statistics on sector wise break up of NPAs (NPAs are Non Performing Assets of banks or delinquent loans to put in more ordinary words) but from my experience I do believe that NPA stuck up with big business houses is much more than the total NPA with the farm and weaker sector.

Further, the latter neither have the availability of services of qualified chartered accountants or lawyers nor the knowledge and resource to avail of whatever legal protection is available to them from the coercive and unlimited recovery and harassment procedure available to the moneylender (albeit Institutional, this time).

Committees and Groups formed for improvement of Agricultural Credit invariably consist of practicing bankers (The moneylenders), and not representatives of small farmers.

This is very much akin to the committees and groups of the British government which tried to manage the affairs of the Indian peasants and artisans during the British rule in which those farmers and artisans had no representation or say in the committees.

Whose interest will these committees watch and protect?

Of farmers, or of their shareholders?

> *Poor returns to cultivation and absence of non-farm opportunities are indicative of the larger socio-economic malaise in rural India. This is accentuated by the multiple risks that the farmer faces – yield, price, input, technology and credit among others. The increasing incidence of farmers' suicides is symptomatic of a larger crisis, which is much more widespread.*
>
> (Mishra, 2007)

7 BANK LOAN AND THE DOWNTRODDEN IN UTTAR PRADESH

After independence, on the realisation that the main impediment in boosting agricultural production in the country was the unavailability of timely finance for the poor agricultural population and the tight grip on them of the traditional moneylender, major banks were nationalised and were systematically brought into play for giving loans to this sector. Many government-supported schemes for providing margin money or part of the interest burden in the form of subsidies were also launched.

It was felt at that time that banks were hesitant in risking their money on agriculture and weaker sectors of the economy. To strengthen their confidence different measures were taken. One of these measures was the formulation of special acts for recovery of such money by different state governments.

The nationalisation of banks, no doubt has resulted in a support for these people and definitely has brought about a relative improvement in the scene; but, on the other hand, has also brought further and new miseries in its turn.

1. The well known and oft talked about of these miseries is eating away of the share or even full of the government subsidies by corrupt officials. Others include insufficient funding of the project, untimely and delayed release of the funds etc.

2. Another area on which probably nothing has been written so far, and which has not at all been talked about, is the presence of harsh and coercive recovery laws which are biased and discriminate grossly against bank borrowers from the agricultural and weaker sectors. Such laws are also misused and abused, by bankers and state recovery officials through the

instrument of Recovery Certificates under (a) UP Public Money (Recovery of Dues Act) and (b) UP Agricultural Credit Act.

The second area is specially the one where I wish to focus, in the light of my very personal memories as an agricultural officer in one of the biggest nationalised banks posted at different levels of control and having interacted directly with the poor borrowers, with the recovery agency i.e., recovery *amins* and *tehsildars,* etc – memories of discussions held at different official meetings right from the BLBC (Block Level Banker's Committee) to SLBC (State Level Bankers Committee) and those gathered during my stint as a functional manager at the zonal office dealing with non-performing assets (i.e., bad loans).

A recovery certificate or RC as it is commonly known is a letter from the bank branch to the district magistrate stating that such and such person availed a loan from the said bank branch, which has gone bad and irrecoverable. Upon receipt of this letter (without any independent enquiry into the allegation, and the circumstances thereto), the district magistrate orders the concerned *tehsildar* to recover the money as dues of land revenue along with a 10% recovery charge and remit it to the bank (The recovery charge goes to government treasury). In the case of non-payment, the recovery *amin* is empowered to arrest the person and the *tehsildar* can imprison the person for a certain term and or confiscate his or her movable and immovable assets.

Who is Covered Under these Acts?

Not the big or medium borrowers, only the following categories:

Under Agriculture Credit Act: All loans and advances given by banks for the purpose of direct agriculture and allied activities like dairy, poultry, piggery etc.

Under UP Public Money (Recovery of dues) Act: Any government supported financial help scheme to the weaker sector of society which has been covered under the scheme through a Government Notification examples are IRDP, Special Component Plan (for the SC/ST beneficiaries), Margin Money Loan Scheme for Minority Communities etc.

At this stage I do not have statistics to support my assertion but I am sure if a caste and community-wise break-up, of the total RCs filed during say last ten years, were collected (and of course, randomly cross checked on surprise check basis) it can be proved beyond doubt that the major chunk of the people affected consists of *Dalits*, Minorities, Women, and other segments of weaker sectors.

Who is the authority to sign RC?

In theory the branch manager.

In practice the loan clerk.

There are instances when only the names of a few alleged defaulters are given to the recovery *amin* by the loan clerk of the bank and he starts recovery, and more than that, harassment of the alleged defaulters even without waiting for an order from the district magistrate.

Has the alleged defaulter, a legal remedy if he has been wrongly framed and harassed?

In theory yes he can go to the court.

In practice, only those go to the court who are moneyed and influential people aware of their right and who have access to and can afford a lawyer to challenge the RC.

Do you expect that a widow whose last piece of land has been snatched against her alleged dues to a bank by the district authority, and who has ultimately again borrowed from the village money lender to eat her bread will go to the court for an appeal?

In fact, even the principle of natural justice (According to which every accused human being has a right to be heard before being punished for any alleged default or crime) is thrown to winds, in the case of an RC.

Is there any mechanism to verify whether the filed RC was correct?

No, in practice there is none!

No RC is ever verified by the district authorities to check whether it was correct or not at any level! It will not be out of place to note and add that in most of the cases a loan goes bad because of the callous approach of the banker – insufficient funding, untimely release of funds, apathy towards providing consumption need support loan (Though there is provision for the same in the RBI directives and most of the bank schemes) in time of family crisis etc, (Not to speak of malicious eating away of subsidy funds – when they were available. Now most of the subsidies have also been withdrawn by the government.)

Is the assumption that banks have a large chunk of their funds locked up in bad credit to agriculture and weaker sector credit true?

In my opinion, not at all! It is just the other way round. The maximum amount of bad loans is locked up with very large enterprises and business houses which play with this money. This can be verified by collecting the necessary information from the banks.

I assume that properly collected and analysed data will make it amply clear that bankers do not need any *specific* protection for their exposure of funds to agriculture and weaker sector. They should be better advised to concentrate on not letting their big accounts utilise the borrowed funds, wrongly.

It is the responsibility of every enlightened citizen, who believes in rule of law, to strive for formation of a body which randomly checks and verifies filed RCs and in case of any instance found fit for a legal challenge, to help and assist the person to fight his case to the end – even if that means going to the Apex Court and to see that all guilty of this misery are duly punished under proper legal framework.

8 THE EAST INDIA COMPANY

> *One of the very first Indian words to enter the English language was the Hindustani slang for plunder: "loot". According to the Oxford English Dictionary, this word was rarely heard outside the plains of north India until the late 18th century, when it suddenly became a common term across Britain.*
>
> (Dalrymple, 2015)

The East India Company was the precursor of the present day corporate business houses. In the words of Robins: *The East India Company can be seen as the mother of the modern corporation, pioneering the modern joint-stock model of financing, as well as the transnational systems of business administration and governance.* (Robins, 2008)

In 1600 when the East India Company got its first charter, its primary objective was to earn profits (maximise wealth?) from overseas trade. In the beginning, when it started trading in India there was hardly any British product it could sell in India in order to purchase the Indian farmers' and artisans' products. The Company thus was given an authorisation to take gold and silver and coins of these metals to India worth £30,000 per annum. The entrepreneurs of The Company, however, did not like the idea of paying gold and silver for the Indian produce (Puri & Misra, 2015).

But The Company eventually seized political power and was able to tilt the balance of exchange in its favour and secure maximum goods for minimum payment.

The margin between trade and plunder, which was never very sharply drawn (the original 'adventurers' often combined trade with piracy) from the very beginning, began to grow conspicuously thin.

The merchant in any case, always favourably placed in relation to the individual producer, whether weaver or peasant, to dictate terms favourable to himself, was now able to throw the sword into the scales to secure a bargain which abandoned all pretence of equality of exchange (Dutt, 1970).

The East India Company used land revenue too as an instrument to loot the Indian farmers. When Cornwallis introduced the permanent settlement in 1793, the land revenue was fixed at £34,00,000, which was meant neither to be spent on administration nor on public welfare in India. The surplus of this revenue was rather repatriated to England as the profit of The Company In the first six years of its administration alone The Company booked a net surplus of £40,37,000 from Bengal only (Puri & Misra, 2015).

After acquiring the *Diwani* rights for the civil administration of Bengal, Bihar and Orissa, the Company started raising land revenue regularly in these provinces. It will not be out of context to quote the following story about acquisition of the *Diwani* rights by the Company:

The painting at Powis that shows the granting of the Diwani is suitably deceptive: the painter, Benjamin West, had never been to India. Even at the time, a reviewer noted that the mosque in the background bore a suspiciously strong resemblance "to our venerable dome of St Paul". In reality, there had been no grand public ceremony. The transfer took place privately, inside Clive's tent, which had just been erected on the parade ground of the newly seized Mughal fort at Allahabad. As for Shah Alam's silken throne, it was, in fact, Clive's armchair, which for the occasion had been hoisted onto his dining room table and covered with a chintz bedspread.

Later, the British dignified the document by calling it the Treaty of Allahabad, though Clive had dictated the terms and a terrified Shah Alam had simply waved them through. As the contemporary Mughal historian Sayyid Ghulam Husain Khan put it: "A business of such magnitude, as left neither pretence nor subterfuge, and which at any other time would have required the sending of wise ambassadors and able negotiators, as well as much parley and conference with the East India Company and the King of England, and much negotiation and contention with the ministers, was done and finished in less time than would usually have been taken up for the sale of a jackass, or a beast of burden, or a head of cattle."
(Dalrymple, 2015)

As a result, the Company generated unexpected surplus on one hand and on the other, the Indian agriculture and farmers were completely ruined slowly destroying their ability to pay the increased revenue, and thus as a long-term guarantee for Company profits, Cornwallis introduced the *Zamindari* system under the permanent settlement in 1793 ensuring a fixed annual land revenue of £34,00,000. The *Zamindars* thus developed a vested interest in the rule of the East India Company.

The flow of Indian capital to England made a great contribution to the success of the industrial revolution, there. But now the industrial revolution required a change in the mode of exploitation. For example, in order to protect the new textile industry in England from much superior hand woven Indian textile, the entrepreneurs made the government impose a heavy customs duty of 78% on import of Indian products into England and to keep British products imported in India, duty-free.

The British capitalists and entrepreneurs had little interest in establishing manufacturing industries in India. They established only such industries here which could not be established elsewhere for geographical reasons – the most prominent was the jute industry established in Bengal, giving them a virtual monopoly in international jute product market thus resulting in huge profits. Other than jute they were interested in tea, coffee and indigo plantation industry, providing them scope for limitless exploitation of local farm workers. In order to protect the interest of the British capitalist entrepreneurs the government always considered it necessary to maintain a big army. In the nineteenth century, the expenditure on the army was the largest single item in government expenditure and accounted for roughly 33% of it. The expenditure on the British army stationed in India was to be borne by the Indian government.

Pensions of army officers, expenditure on the office of the Secretary of State for India, salaries of the members of the Indian Council, expenditure on the India Office, and payments to the Bank of England for debt management were some other expenditure which had little to do with the development, protection or well-being of the local peasant or artisan.

The exploitation of India by the British industrial capital in the nineteenth century brought about a drastic change in the nature of the Indian Economy. The isolation of self-sufficient villages ended and with it the old form of economy disintegrated. In urban areas, the process of de-industrialisation was more or less complete. The earlier balance which existed between agriculture and industry in this country during the pre-British period was also lost (Puri & Misra, 2015).

In the mid-nineteenth century, a period of massive investment of *British* capital in India began. But this capital was not brought from England. The capital plundered from the people of India was invested as British capital. The public debt system was another crafty device employed to raise funds. L. H. Jenks wrote: *The burdens that it was convenient to charge to India seems preposterous. The cost of the Mutiny, the price of the transfer of the Company's right to the Crown, the expenses of simultaneous wars in China and Abyssinia, every government item in London that related to India down to the fees of the char-woman in the India Office and expenses of ships that sail out but did not participate in hostilities and the cost of Indian Regiments for six month training in home before they sailed – all were charged to the account of unrepresented ryot... It is small wonder that the Indian revenue swelled from £33 million to £52 million a year during the first thirteen years of Crown administration...* (Puri & Misra, 2015).

The decline in real wages of both skilled and unskilled workers in 1928 was roughly 50% of what they were in 1807. The wages of unskilled workers were not even 40% of what they were in 1807. (*ibid*).

There is virtually no statistical information on poverty in India for the first hundred years of British rule. The descriptive information in official documents and other writings of the period is, however, quite revealing. On the basis of these sources, it has been conclusively proved that India was far more prosperous during the pre – British period than the contemporary Europe. No doubt Indian nobles, government officials and urban traders were steeped in luxury and comfort, but farmers and artisans did not suffer from starvation. (ibid).

This is a brief account of the East India Company, the precursor of the corporates becoming interested in the Indian market with good business sense, not a sense of do-gooding and as a result, what they did to the Indian economy. The entrepreneur capitalist in the infancy of The Company directly plundered Indian people first and then through the Crown. This experiment taught their successors the lesson that for them it was more economical and convenient to loot, not directly, but through the state. And the lesson learnt continues to be practised, not in India alone, but in the entire world.

The British government, guarding the interest of its capitalist entrepreneurs, quickly learnt that in order to keep the attention of the exploited local people away from the real exploiters, it was necessary to divide them into factions, into religious and communal lines and pit them against each other. They succeeded in their endeavour so much that when they left India, they left it divided into two parts politically and three, geographically, amidst a huge blood bath and untold sentimental pains and human misery.

It is a saga of good business sense devoid of a sense of do-gooding, which resulted in the formation of the wealth pyramid with its base in India and other similar countries where today half of the world population lives on less than $2 per head per day, and with its narrow tip situated in the west where most of the 1% of the global population controlling 50% of world's wealth dwell.

Invite the successors of the Company again to the base of the pyramid, which is the largest *market chunk*, with a good business sense, not a sense of do-gooding and the last drop of the life blood of people here will be sucked by the big octopus – the corporates for wealth maximisation of their equity shareholders.

Picture 2 A cannon at British Residency at Lucknow, which was used to blow locals who opposed the hegemony of East India Company in 1857. (*Photo: Masood Rezvi*)

The prisoner is generally tied to a gun with the upper part of the small of his back resting against the muzzle. When the gun is fired, his head is seen to go straight up into the air some forty or fifty feet; the arms fly off right and left, high up in the air, and fall at, perhaps, a hundred yards distance; the legs drop to the ground beneath the muzzle of the gun; and the body is literally blown away altogether, not a vestige being seen.

(Havholm, 2008)

9 ECONOMIC 'REFORMS' AND FARMER SUICIDES

Over 50 years since independence, India made immense progress towards food security.

Prior to the mid-1960s, India relied on imports and food aid to meet domestic requirements. However, two years of severe drought in 1965 and 1966 convinced India to reform agricultural policy, and that India could not rely on foreign aid and foreign imports for food security. India adopted significant policy reforms focused on the goal of food grain self-sufficiency.

As a result, though Indian population tripled, but food-grain production more than quadrupled, thanks to the relentless efforts of agricultural scientists and farmers and the government policies supporting agriculture in defining it as the first and foremost segment of the priority sector of Indian economy.

But, a 2003 analysis of India's agricultural growth from 1970 to 2001 by the Food and Agriculture Organisation identified systemic problems in Indian agriculture. For food staples, the annual growth rate in production during the six-year segments 1970-76, 1976–82, 1982–88, 1988–1994, 1994-2000 were found to be respectively 2.5, 2.5, 3.0, 2.6, and 1.8% per annum. Corresponding analyses for the index of total agricultural production show a similar pattern, with the growth rate for 1994-2000 attaining only 1.5% per annum.

It is evident that the decline in the growth rate corresponds with the ushering in of the era of economic 'reforms' in the early nineties!

Inequality has reached one of the highest rates India has ever seen. In a report by Chetan Ahya, of Morgan Stanley, it is pointed out that there has been a wealth increase of close to $1 trillion in the time frame of 2003–2007 in the Indian stock market while only 4%–7% of the Indian population hold any equity. During the time when public investment in agriculture shrank to 2% of the GDP, the nation suffered the worst agrarian crisis in decades, the same time as India became the nation with the second highest number of dollar billionaires. Farm incomes have collapsed. Hunger has grown very fast. Public investment in agriculture shrank to nothing a long time ago. (weebly.com).

The per capita food availability has declined every five years without exception from 1992–2010 whereas from 1972–1991 it had risen every five-year period without exception. (Rohan).

In fact, the 1989 – 92 period, is very, very important in Indian history and can never be forgotten.

At one hand the Indian government was under immense pressure from IMF and the western world for what is known as 'economic reforms' and on the other a very serious communal strife was brewing up in the entire country between Hindus and the largest religious minority, the Muslims with its epicentre at Ayodhya in Faizabad district of Uttar Pradesh over a place of worship. Though the contention was ages old it systematically became the single most important public issue, during this period. This was the biggest communal contention after the conflict that resulted in the partition of India at the eve of her independence.

The Ayodhya conflict was so intense that the entire machinery of public life in India became mentally a hostage to it, be it the parliament, the government, the media, the police and law enforcing agencies, the intellectuals, whether Hindu or Muslim or professing another faith or atheist. Even the maximum time of judiciary and the bar was devoted to lawsuits related to this dispute.

Was the chronological concurrence of Ayodhya dispute with economic reforms a mere coincidence, or was it a dexterously designed and planned move on the chess board of Indian macroeconomic transformation, to keep the media, the intelligentsia and the public at large engrossed in it and away from thinking anything about the process and pros and cons of the reforms? I keep on wondering, and will be immensely grateful if someone could give me a convincing reply.

While this chapter was being penned down, one of the saddest incidents of Indian history took place in a village called Dadri which is only about 50 KMs away from the national capital and is situated in the state of Uttar Pradesh. A farm worker, Mr. Akhlaque was pulled out of his house at around 10:30 PM on the night of 29th September 2015 and lynched to death while his son Danish was seriously injured by a group of Hindu fanatics over a rumour that he ate beef (BBC News, 2015). The cow is a sacred animal for Hindus and Mr. Akhlaque was a Muslim. The incident had all the potential of a massive communal flare up, which thanks to the netizens' vocal protest on social media and the intervention of the intellectual class mainly Hindus in favour of Mr. Akhlaque, was averted. Sad as the incident was, it prima facie did not merit a mention here but a Facebook post by one of my seasoned journalist friends Mr. Ashish Tripathi compelled me into searching more about the village Dadri and its history which so far had no record of a Hindu-Muslim conflict.

This is what I found:

The National Human Rights Commission took cognizance of a complaint of unprovoked lathicharge, firing and pelting of stones by the police on 7th and 8th July-2006 on the villagers of Ghaziabad District who were protesting against acquisition of their farmlands and habitats in the name of the mega development project. As per the petition submitted by Justice Rajender Sachar, former President PUCL, and others, the land of seven villages in Ghaziabad district measuring about 2500 acres was acquired by the State for the Reliance Power Project in Dadri. The affected villagers were awarded a meagre compensation of ₹150/- ($2.32 at October 2015 conversion rate) per sq. yard for their lands though the prevailing price was somewhere around ₹500/- ($7.72 at October 2015 conversion rate) per sq. yard. It is alleged that when the villagers on realizing the unfair deal meted out to them indulged in protests, the Chief Minister, UP assured them that they would get compensation at the rate of ₹300/- (($4.63 at October 2015 conversion rate) per sq. yard. However, the promise was not fulfilled. Upon which the villagers resorted to peaceful protest. During the course of the protest, they were *beaten by the police, injuring several villagers. Two more petitions by – Dr. Vandana Shiva, Founder Director, Research Foundation for Science, Technology and Ecology, New Delhi and by Ms. Meera Singh Sengar, State General Secretary, UP Mahila Congress (I) Committee were also received by the Commission in this regard. Taking cognizance of the complaint, the Commission sought a factual report from the Chief Secretary and DGP, UP as also a response from the DM on the allegations of police highhandedness.*

Even as the response of the State Government was awaited, Shri V. P. Singh and others visited the Commission on September 19, 2006, and submitted a petition alleging another incident which took place on September 17, 2006, in which more than 15 people including women and old persons suffered serious injuries. The petitioners requested NHRC to send its inquiry team to inquire into the events of 7th & 8th July 2006 and also of 17th September-2006 to fix the responsibility and initiate action against the police officials found guilty. The Commission while considering all the petitions submitted before it observed that it appears that genesis of the alleged incidents, as per the allegations in the complaints, lies in the acquisition of land/habitats of the villagers for a mega power project. The complaints raise a serious issue relating to relocation and rehabilitation of the persons displaced by the project. The Commission thus requested the Chief Secretary, UP to furnish, within six weeks, whether any plan had been formulated for compensation and rehabilitation of the persons dislocated from their habitats/lands for mega development projects, and if so, whether any plan had been formulated for relocation and rehabilitation of the persons affected by the acquisition of land for Reliance Power Project. (National Human Rights Commission, 2006).

Four thousand eight hundred and forty square yards make an acre. So, our government procured each of the 2500 acres of land from farmers for Reliance, one of the biggest Indian corporate houses at a mere $4840 \times 2.32 = \$11,211.62$ per acre in the suburbs of the national capital!

I am not aware as to what finally happened of this complaint. But now after the beef rumour lynching case, at least, the local farmers are divided, guilt-ridden, and implicated and involved in another issue, quite different from the price of their land to be paid by the government and the corporate house.

Earlier, a united farmer community fought against state-sponsored loot. Today, people are being made to fight among themselves in the name of religion. (Tripathi, 2015).

In U.P., the proposed eight expressways and the townships planned along the route, along with land being gobbled by other industrial, real estate and investment projects are likely to eat away more than 23,000 villages, one-fourth of the total number of villages.

Former Agriculture Minister Ajit Singh has in a statement said that one-third of the total cultivable land of Uttar Pradesh will be eventually acquired. The state government neither denies nor confirms this, but acknowledges that land diversion is 'large'.

This means that out of the total area of 19.8 million hectares under food grain crops in Uttar Pradesh, one-third or roughly 6.6 million hectares will be shifted from agriculture to non-agriculture activity. Much of the fertile and productive lands of western Uttar Pradesh will, therefore, disappear, to be replaced by concrete jungles.

As per rough estimates, 6.6 million hectares that would be taken out of farming would mean a production loss of 14 million tons of food grains. In other words, Uttar Pradesh will be faced with a terrible food crisis in the years to come, the seeds for which are being sown now. Add to this the anticipated shortfall in potato and sugarcane production, since the area under these two crops will also go down drastically, the road ahead for Uttar Pradesh is not only dark but also laced with social unrest.

Already a part of the BIMARU states (the worst performing states as far as economic indices are concerned); Uttar Pradesh will surely see a surge in hunger, malnutrition and under-nourishment. I shudder to imagine the socio-economic and political fallout of the misadventure that the government is attempting with such a massive land takeover (Singh C. B., 2011).

The large discretionary role of the state in the process of land acquisition, conversion and diversion serves the interests of both politicians and the private sector. For politicians, and sometimes bureaucrats, it can carry large economic payoffs as well as serving developmental purposes. For the private sector, going through the government rather than negotiating directly with farmers can be advantageous, especially where large tracts of land are concerned. (Chandra K., 2015).

In India, the instances of political parties supporting and acting as a corporate group's strongmen are not rare! (Tiwari & Pandey, 2013).

Doesn't the beef rumour lynching case of Dadri merit a mention on these pages?

The post-reform India saw a growth in GDP and a new breed of billionaires on one hand and a quite new phenomenon of a spiralling number of farmer suicides. The huge wave of farm suicides in Indian rural population from 1997 to 2007 totalled close to 200,000 according to official statistics (Singh C. B., 2011). The number remains disputed; with some saying the true number is much higher. As journalist P Sainath of *The Hindu*, describes in his reports on the rural economy in India, the level of inequality has risen to extraordinary levels, when at the same time, hunger in India has reached its highest level in decades, rural economies across India have collapsed, or are on the verge of collapse due to the neo-liberal policies of the government of India since the 1990s. In 2012, the National Crimes Records Bureau of India reported 13,754 farmer suicides (National Crime Reports Bureau, 2012), and if we believe what *Aljazeera* has reported, 41 farmers commit suicide in India every day (Umar, 2015)!

The post-2007 story has shown almost no improvement.

One of the main reasons for these suicides has been reported by almost all the researchers to be the debt trap – the trap created as a result or by-product of banking companies along with the local moneylenders going after this big chunk of the market at the bottom of the pyramid with a good business sense, not a sense of do-gooding!

Can the situation be reversed?

10 THE REALITY SHOWS

Each possession you possess

Helps your spirits to soar

That's what's soothing about excess

Never settle for something less

Something's better than nothing, yes

But nothing's better than more, more, more

(Except all, all, all)

Except all, all, all

(Madonna, 1990)

Their reality show, *Sa Re Ga Ma* (2007) aired by the Zee TV, proved to be a great success. This show was organised to search the "Voice of the World" or the best singer of Hindustani songs.

The show also had a philanthropic angle as Poonam, a girl from a very ordinary middle class family at Lucknow – who, as was repeatedly informed during the episodes, earned a mere ₹600/- ($9.27 at the conversion rate today) per month from her job at a public call office at Lucknow – was one of the participants. She received a lot of sympathy from the anchor, the gurus, and most important of all, the viewers. Raja Hasan from Rajasthan also came from a very humble middle-class family. Amanat definitely remained a symbol of goodwill and friendship between India and Pakistan and was religiously supported by all those who believe in goodwill and peace. The Royal Cub of Bengal, the voice of the world the winner Aneek Dhar, represented the sweet melodious voice so typical of Bengal.

It was really very interesting to note that most of the major TV channels in India gave the show full publicity and news coverage, putting aside all professional rivalry.

Like millions of other middle-class people, my wife remained glued to the TV during all episodes of *Sa Re Ga Ma*. Whenever I had a chance of viewing the performance of those energy charged young boys and girls I too watched with interest and was charmed by their sweet voices. They all are superb no doubt. I wish them all great success in their career.

The "reality", however, really showed when the enormous number of votes received by these participants was revealed! On 13 October at the grand finale, the show broke voting records with a collection of 10,61,44,354 or 106 plus million votes... Whoops!

Since I did not vote for any, I wondered how much it costs a voter to cast one such vote on phone or SMS. Some said ten rupees per vote others said six rupees per vote some others said no it was just three rupees an SMS. I could not verify the figures for myself and, therefore, put it at the lowest that is three rupees per vote. Thus, the money earned by the telecom corporate houses put together for the mega finale episode alone was 318 million rupees plus, or around $4.91 million plus.

Congratulations to all participating corporate houses and their brilliant managers!

Interestingly one of the methods available for voting was through email but if you chose that method you were allowed to cast one vote only per person/machine, while if you used your mobile for the voting you could cast an unlimited number of votes. The reason is so simple. No corporate earns when you shoot an email. While with every SMS the service provider takes out a small chunk of money from the pocket of its customer. Had they genuinely wanted to know the popularity of the participants, they could have limited the voting to one vote from one cell phone it was very easy from a technical point of view. But they did not! They encouraged youngsters, a large chunk of them from the bottom of the pyramid or a little above the bottom, to go crazy with the frenzy of sending as many SMS each for their favourite as they could, or in other words to throw three rupee coins in the bag of the corporate houses as quickly as possible.

The job of telecom companies is to provide communication services to the people and to fulfil their perceived needs for communication. Is it fair for them, by any standard, to artificially stoke a fire of frenzy among the children and adolescents, a large chunk of whom comprised of bottom of the pyramid segment, specially because of their sympathy with Poonam etc., to push them to spend money relentlessly and without check, the purpose of which, as is clear, could not be knowing how many people favoured a particular contestant, but of how much, the supporters of a particular contestant were ready to pay to the telecom service providers!

And remember the figures I have quoted here, are for the mega finale episode only. I could not find out the total number of votes for all episodes put together. Was it 200 million votes? Was it 300 million votes? Or was it 1000 million votes? I do not know!

Was that not an organized assault on the pockets of the bottom of the pyramid people by those at the top of the pyramid, and their b-school graduated managers?

This is precisely what will happen if the businesses will go after the large chunk of the market at the bottom of the pyramid, with a good business sense and not a sense of do-gooding.

I call it a process of reverse osmosis.

Whenever the top of the pyramid is connected with the bottom with good business sense and not a sense of do-gooding, money starts flowing against the gradient. Or, in other words, is sucked from the bottom to the top, and then to the top of the top, thus giving the pyramid its typical shape.

> *Every so often, it takes one isolated instance of misdemeanour to spark off renewed demands for improved corporate governance. The need is felt more acutely in times of slowing demand; when the going is good, caution and, indeed, good corporate governance is thrown to the winds. Everybody swims along with the tide, and the whistleblowers are branded society's curmudgeons.*
>
> (Singhal, 2008)

11 THE DILEMMA OF CORPORATE GOVERNANCE AND SCAMS

There has been a renewed interest in the corporate governance practices of modern corporations, particularly in relation to accountability, since the high-profile collapses of a number of large corporations during 2001–2002, most of which involved accounting fraud; and then again after the later financial crisis in 2008. Corporate scandals of various forms have maintained public and political interest in the regulation of corporate governance.

In the U.S., these include Enron and MCI Inc. (Formerly WorldCom). Their demise is associated with the U.S. federal government passing the Sarbanes-Oxley Act in 2002, intending to restore public confidence in corporate governance. Comparable failures in Australia (HIH, One.Tel) are associated with the eventual passage of the CLERP 9 reforms. (Lee & Shailer, 2008).

Corporate governance broadly refers to the mechanisms, processes and relations by which corporations are controlled and directed. (Shailer, 2004).

In India – *Corporate governance is the acceptance by management of the inalienable rights of shareholders as the true owners of the corporation and of their own role as trustees on behalf of the shareholders. It is about commitment to values, about ethical business conduct and about making a distinction between personal and corporate funds in the management of a company.* (Securities and Exchange Board of India, 2013).

For a lay person like me, and perhaps like you, all that sounds very complicated and esoteric. So what is corporate governance all about? How is it related to failures of corporations? Why should be it mentioned in a book on poverty? Why are shareholders the true owners of the corporation and the managers, trustee? What is ethical business conduct?

There were times when doing business was rather quite simple. There was a capitalist cum entrepreneur cum manager cum artisan or artist or craftsman cum owner who used to produce artefacts with his own capital and family labour and keep the residual fruits of its sale proceed with him and his family. In this type of business, the *owner* was the *manager*.

With the advent of corporations, the ownership was divided into small portions of owners' fund called equity and subscribed by many hundred or thousands of shareholders. Naturally it no longer remained feasible for all the owners to oversee and manage the day to day business. Corporate business is therefore managed by managers – the top ones elected by the shareholders and others hired by the top ones. The top ones are generally also holders of a part but not all of the share capital or equity. A major part of the share capital is however generally contributed by others, i.e., other than the managers. The managers, therefore, manage the business as trustees or agents of others too. What ought to be their responsibility as agents?

In Milton Friedman's view corporate executives' *responsibility... generally, will be to make as much money as possible.* (Friedman, 1970).

This gives rise to the maxim of wealth maximisation of shareholders resulting into a three-cornered win-lose distributive situation. A win-lose situation or a situation of distributive bargaining is one in which one party's gain will definitely mean the loss of the other party(s).

The three parties involved in the game are:

i)   The Equity Share Holders

ii)   The Managers and

iii) Other publics (the most ill-organised and helpless) like employees, customers, ecosystem, the community and humanity at large.

Fully trained in the ethics of Friedman and the philosophy of wealth maximisation, the manager, working ethically is supposed to make as much money as possible from the parties listed at point number iii above for the wealth maximisation of party number i. If he or she does so, good corporate governance is in place, till all legal provisions as per the law of the land are complied with, and the corporate house is not caught breaking a law.

On the other hand, the SEBI and its likes teach and preach that the manager should make him or her comfortable with his or her fixed salary only, and should not think of his or her own wealth maximisation. Plain logic will tell us that psychologically it is impossible to apply a norm of highest possible exploitation of all parties, other than the shareholders, for maximising the wealth of shareholders – with the only rider that the corporation is not caught breaking a law – on one hand, and to not to apply the same rule for maximising one's own wealth, on the other.

It is simply this distorted and misplaced value system which is resulting in corporate frauds and scandals. No amount of safeguards and law can prevent or cure the malaise until and unless the basic objective of business is redefined.

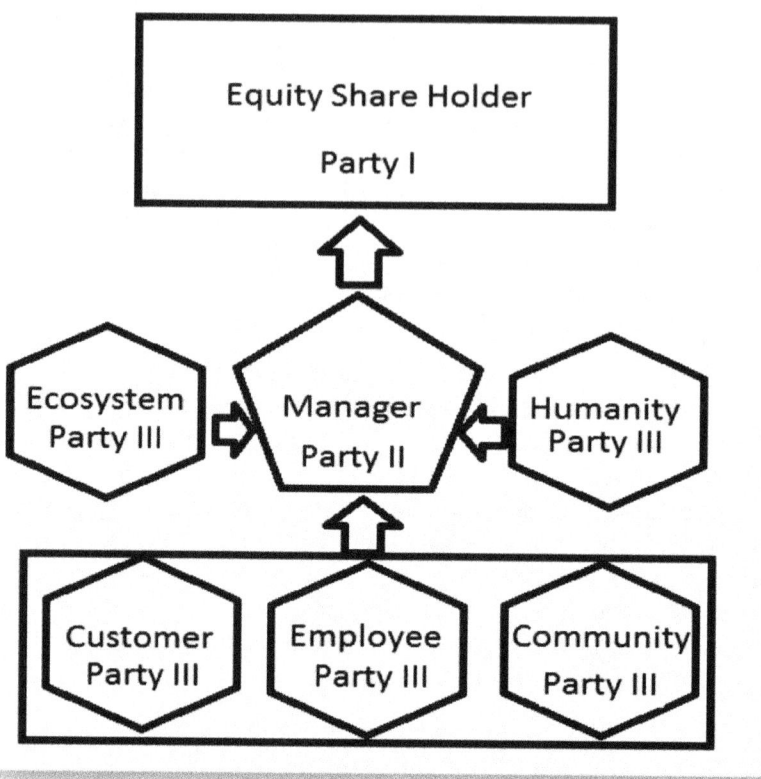

Illustration 3 The three party conflict in corporate governance. Arrows show the flow of money from one party to another. (Illustration: Masood Rezvi)

As regards the working of legal system alone it can hardly be of any service if we believe in a report published in Business Standard (Inamdar, 2013), which lists the following as the *five big Corporate scams pending judgments, in which the under-trial accused continue to roam scot-free, years after cases were filed against them:*

1. *Ketan Parekh Securities Scam (2001) – Parekh was allegedly involved in circular trading and stock manipulation through 1999-2001 in a host of companies. Like Harshad Mehta, Parekh too, it is alleged borrowed from banks like Global Trust Bank and Madhavpura Mercantile Co-operative Bank, and manipulated a host of stocks popularly known as K-10 stocks.*

2. *Home Trade Scam (2002) – A brokerage allegedly embezzling funds from over 25 corporate banks across Maharashtra by luring them with higher interest rates on gilt trading. Investigations revealed that the G-Secs which Home Trade claimed to have bought were not physically delivered and may not have even existed.*

3. *Satyam (2009) – An accounting scandal where the accused confessed to having cooked up the accounts of Satyam Computers and inflated its bank balances.*

4. *Speak Asia Scam (2011) – An online business survey firm that allegedly collected thousands of crores of rupees from over 24 lakh investors, asking them to fill surveys and guaranteeing to quadruple their income in one year, Speak Asia was accused of running a Ponzi scheme. A criminal case was registered against the firm in 2011, some of its accounts were frozen, and its business was shut down.*

5. *Saradha Chit Fund Scam (2013) – One of the biggest Ponzi schemes in West Bengal that allegedly enjoyed political patronage and lured millions of investors to deposit money with the promise of abnormally high returns including fancy holidays etc. The chit fund eventually collapsed leading to defaults after a crackdown by SEBI and the Reserve*

Bank of India. The default, apart from leaving small depositors high and dry, also led to 10 media outlets owned by Saradha being forced to wind up, leaving 1000 journalists jobless.

This is only the tip of the iceberg and must have grown much bigger by now.

Government functionaries and elected representatives of the public, the trustees of law, have not lagged behind in swimming with the tide. Rather with all the powers conferred upon them by the electorate, they have been taking a lead. Even a thin veneer of propriety has been conveniently thrown to the winds as is clear from the most recent Vyapam scandal which has claimed the lives of dozens of people even remotely interested in it. Those who died because of "unnatural causes" include reporting journalists.

One after the other, people variously linked with the Vyapam scam, are dying. The mystery deepens with every new death reported even as the probe agencies struggle to unravel it.

A cursory perusal shows that not only have candidates died but also dummy aspirants as also those probing the scam.

The MP government on June 25 admitted in the high court that 25 accused have died.

However, TOI's investigations put the death toll at 46. (The Times of India, 2015).

Only yesterday on the 17th of October 2015 the Vyapam scam once again came into news after a retired bureaucrat, who was an observer for two recruitment tests connected with the scam, was found dead in Odisha. The body of retired Indian Forest Services (IFS) officer Vijay Bahadur has been found on a railway track in Jharsuguda. (The Indian Express, 2015).

Alas, the rat race for wealth maximisation!

Alas, the sad demise of a sense of do-gooding!

Who knows how much deep we all are going into this abyss?

Who knows whether ever, ever we will be able to come out of it?

A Trail of graft and gore

1982: Vyaysayik Pareeksha Mandel (Vyapam) set up to conduct entrance examinations for professional courses

2008: Recruitment tests for government jobs also included

July 5, 2009: Widespread irregularities in recruitments come to light

2009: Medical exam paper leaked; first complaint filed

December, 2009: Chief Minister forms panel to probe scam

Jul 7, 2013: Police register FIR, arrest 20 impersonators

Jul 16, 2013: Jag-dish Sagar, kingpin of scam, arrested

Aug 26, 2013: STF takes over probe, 55 FIRs registered

Oct 9, 2013: Admissions of 345 examinees cancelled

Dec 18,2013: Ex-Higher Education Minister Laxmikant Sharma booked

Jun 29, 2015: SIT says 23 people related to scam died due to "Unnatural causes"; unofficial count puts figure at 46

July 7: Chouhan agrees to CBI probe

Table 1 The Vyapam calendar (The Hindu, 2015)

> *People of the same trade seldom meet together, even for merriment and diversion, but the conversation ends in a conspiracy against the public, or in some contrivance to raise prices.*
>
> (Smith, 1776/1952)

12 CORPORATE SOCIAL RESPONSIBILITY

According to United Nations Industrial Development Organization (UNIDO), Corporate Social Responsibility (CSR) is a management concept whereby companies integrate social and environmental concerns in their business operations and interactions with their stakeholders. CSR is generally understood as being the way through which a company achieves a balance of economic, environmental and social imperatives ("Triple-Bottom-Line-Approach") while at the same time addressing the expectations of shareholders and stakeholders. In this sense, it is important to draw a distinction between CSR, which can be a strategic business management concept, and charity, sponsorships or philanthropy. Even though the latter can also make a valuable contribution to poverty reduction, will directly enhance the reputation of a company and strengthen its brand, the concept of CSR clearly goes beyond that.

It is an attempt to align private enterprises to the goal of sustainable global development by providing them with a more comprehensive set of working objectives than just profit alone. The perspective taken is that for an organization to be sustainable, it must be financially secure, minimise (or ideally eliminate) its negative environmental impacts and act in conformity with societal expectations.

This sounds a healthy departure from Friedman's advocacy of wealth maximisation, more candidly preached by Madonna through her song – *Once upon a time I had plenty of nothing.*

Confederation of Indian Industries (CII) describes CSR in India as follows: *The Companies Act, 2013 has introduced the idea of CSR to the forefront and through its disclose-or-explain mandate, is promoting greater transparency and disclosure.*

Schedule VII of the Act, which lists out the CSR activities, suggests communities to be the focal point. On the other hand, by discussing a company's relationship with its stakeholders and integrating CSR into its core operations, the draft rules suggest that CSR needs to go beyond communities and beyond the concept of philanthropy. It will be interesting to observe the ways in which this will translate into action at the ground level, and how the understanding of CSR is set to undergo a change. (CII, 2013).

Business News Daily has the following advice to offer in this regard: *Undertaking socially responsible initiatives is truly a win-win situation. Not only will your company appeal to socially conscious consumers and employees, but you'll also make a real difference in the world. Keep in mind that in CSR, transparency and honesty about what you're doing are paramount to earning the public's trust. "If decisions [about social responsibility] are made behind closed doors, people will wonder if there are strings attached, and if the donations are really going where they say," Cooney said. "Engage your employees [and consumers] in giving back. Let them feel like they have a voice."*

The same newspaper identifies key CSR issues as environmental management, eco-efficiency, responsible sourcing, stakeholder engagement, labour standards and working conditions, employee and community relations, social equity, gender balance, human rights, good governance, and anti-corruption measures. (Fallon, 2015).

Incidentally, companies with no past experience of CSR, end up adopting a check-list approach. Under the head of CSR, smaller firms are adopting questionable practices like tying up with nongovernmental organisations (NGOs) run by friends and families. There are instances of CSR funds being diverted to sponsorships of activities done by people known or related to the executives of the company. (Somwanshi, 2015).

August 29, 2013, was a red-letter day in the field of Indian corporate Law when the Companies Act 2013 was enacted with the aim of improving and simplifying corporate governance norms and legislate the role of whistle-blowers. (Rakesh, 2015).

The basic principle of corporate responsibility is said to involve such responsible business practices which are ethical in nature, and practices which respect and recognize human rights, fair sourcing and protection of the environment.

This seems to be a contentious issue because it is rightly argued by the critics that the companies may try to adopt camouflaging activities to meet these regulations, particularly during an economic downturn. Also, some have stated this to be an act of outsourcing governance wherein the government has shouldered their responsibility to the companies. (*ibid*)

The absence of any prescribed penalties in case any company fails to comply or set aside two percent of Net profits for CSR is another grey area since it is not clear whether any company can get away from non-compliance simply by disclosing reasons for not spending mandatory amount or would they be liable to pay any sort of penalties. This is said to be a major setback due to an absence of a deterrent force to curb fraudulent practices. Similarly, there is an absence of clearly laid down powers, duties and responsibilities of the Committee entrusted to carry out the CSR policy and this leads to the failure of purpose with which the framework was set up by any company. (ibid)

"Contributions to PM's national relief fund and such other funds established by the central or state government" as one of the activities to be taken up under CSR as prescribed under Schedule VIII poses another challenge since it is argued to be deeply flawed. It is believed that such an activity is subject to misuse as the funds so raised are not accountable. Besides this, as per the submission of the Prime Minister's Office (PMO) to the Central Information Commission, the Prime Minister's National Relief Fund itself is not a Government body. (ibid)

Now let me share with you a personal experience. In March 2015, I was invited to participate and speak at a workshop on corporate social responsibility at one of the private management colleges at the outskirts of Lucknow. The workshop was sponsored by the appropriate ministry in the central government and was mainly being handled by an NGO specialising in the subject. There were some representatives, a couple of them Americans, of an MNC too.

The main speaker who was introduced as a pioneer researcher on corporate social responsibility in India gave a detailed talk on what corporate social responsibility was about. He said that corporate social responsibility revolved around three Ps, Profit, People and Planet and elaborated the subject at great length mainly for the benefit of the MBA students present in the workshop.

When I was invited to speak, I humbly differed with the learned authority on two issues. Firstly, I said, that the order of the Ps may kindly be changed. It should be made Planet, People, and Profit, because first there was the planet. Then people emerged on it as a distinct form of life different from other forms in many ways in their behaviour, and then only came the concept of a capitalist entrepreneur appropriating the residual benefit of an endeavour after paying a fixed amount to other factors of production, which is called the profit. Since profit was the residual amount he always wanted to maximise it which was possible only from two sources either by exploiting the planet and people to the maximum possible or by keeping back and corner cutting what belonged to the owners of the other factors of production by cajoling or coercing them as far as possible to settle for a lesser and lesser fixed reward for their contributions in production; or a mix of these two.

Second, in the era of corporate business, thanks to the *philosophical* preachings of Milton Friedman et al, the new mantra was not profit. It was *wealth* maximisation. Thus, use of the term *profit* while talking about corporate social responsibility was misleading and might be kindly changed appropriately.

On the same morning, I had my personal brush with corporate social (ir)responsibility. I use a prepaid phone connection and have got it duly registered with the national *do not disturb* registry. But I received an SMS sort of *"Dear customer in order to register for our XYZ service please send SMS to such and such number"* I never sent the request for activation of that service. But I received the second one sort of *"Thank you for registering for our XYZ service"*, and lost some money from my available balance as a fee for that XYZ service. The deactivation request was accepted when I called the customer care but the money deducted was never returned.

And this was not the first instance. This had happened to me and to my family members many times earlier too. How was it possible? It was only possible if a bug was deliberately incorporated in the computer programme of the service provider by them to read a confirmatory SMS by default. Now if The Company deducted say ₹30 from 100 thousand customers; they maximised their shareholders' wealth by ₹3000000 in a fraction of a second. None of the customer losing a small amount of ₹30 would do anything except a little whimpering and so the law never came in the way of this innovative wealth maximisation exercise.

After narrating the story, I asked if there was anyone in the audience who had never had this experience. As expected, there was none!

A friend of mine video recorded my talk and sent it to me which in the afternoon I uploaded on YouTube and sent a link of the same to the professor of corporate social responsibility at the host college, who had been kind enough to invite me to the workshop.

By the evening, I received his phone call. After lot of apologies he said that his boss, the head of the NGO which was running the college, who happens to be a real state businessman by profession, wanted that video to be removed from YouTube, because the programme was organised with financial aid from different sources and if it was known to them that such a talk was delivered at such and such college against corporates the college might attract displeasure of high ups and may lose further financial help. The professor further said that he fully agreed with me but I should understand that he was only an employee etc, etc.

I couldn't harm him. So I removed the video.

Merciful Lord! This is a democracy with guaranteed freedom of speech in which we are living!!

> *According to the data released by the Zonal Integrated Police Network under the union ministry, 33,518 homeless people died in Delhi between January 2004 and October 2015.*
>
> (The Times of India, 2015)

13 WHAT TO DO?

Before we try to answer the question – what to do, Let us try summarising what has gone wrong.

And before doing that, we will have to accept that something has gone seriously wrong and that, if we do not wake up in time and start putting in our sincere efforts, despite the most severe odds against us, our home – the planet earth – is doomed to be destroyed and become uninhabitable very soon.

And before we move further let me tell you that the above warning, horrible as it might be, for me and you, does not really bother all people equally. There are some, who think or fantasise that by that time new inhabitable planets or space stations will be discovered or invented and when the planet earth becomes uninhabitable they will be able to move on to these inhabitable worlds or places.

Hard to believe?

Okay, go fetch yourself some sci-fi stuff. My favourite is Isaac Asimov's. You may try others too. Get yourself drowned in the spacer worlds, in the antigravity spaceships, hyperspace jump etc. You will soon find that what is being fantasised (preached?) is a story that the chosen few, will escape to safety in outer space while earth and the rest of the unfortunate inhabitants down here will be doomed to eternal destruction.

In this way, the process of natural selection in the scheme of evolution of a new species will play its role.

The new world – the other world – will be the paradise for those chosen few and this world will become hell for those doomed due to the sin of poverty. Poverty is their sin and they are sinners because they are poor – The new species will be a species of supermen *ubermensch*!

That is why when generously talking about corporate social responsibility, putting the cart in front of horse they arrange the 3Ps of CSR in this order – Profit, People, Planet, while to my mind it should be the other way round that is Planet, People and then Profit. Well, the sequence matters – is rather crucial.

Isn't it?

As we know fifty percent of the world's wealth is controlled by 1% of population only, and this inequality is not static but growing globally (Treanor, 2015), thus in the present scenario, the percentage is not expected to grow from 1% by the inclusion of more people into it. It will rather shrink. The top of the pyramid is getting thinner, sharper and farther away from its bottom.

Thus, there is hardly any chance that people like me and you who belong to the other 99% of world population will ever be able to go to this other world at the time of the destruction of our home, our natural habitat – the planet earth. Looking at the planet as a market and not as the home is okay from the point of the 1% population but cannot be okay from the point of view of the remaining ninety-nine percent.

The idea of the other world and God's chosen people has its origin basically in religious scriptures. But *that* other world is promised after death as salvation, *nirvana, moksha* or *nijah*. Another difference is that the scriptures invariably emphasise on do-gooding and consider do-gooding as the only route to becoming the chosen one of God for all mortals.

Scientific methodology has been unable to find any indication of life after death. But it has no way of disproving or denying it either. For example the scientific methodology, so far known, has failed to prove the existence of extraterrestrial intelligence. But it has neither succeeded in disproving it. That we don't know a thing does not prove that the thing does not exist. That, logically for the premise *we do not know it, thus, it does not exist* to be true, the premise that *we know all that exists* must first be true. And it is beyond any argument and proof and is self-evident that it is not true. We do not know all that exists.

The religious philosophies and points of view look upon the entire globe as a family and not as a market. *Vasudhaiva kutmbakam* – The world is a family – says *Mahopnishad* the sacred Indian book.

Do-gooding was never limited to religious scriptures only. We know staunch atheists who strongly advocated do-gooding and treating the entire humanity as one family. The best known of them was perhaps Karl Marx.

Do-gooding has been documented even in animals like monkeys, ravens and vampire bats which share their food with other members of the species, and this is instinctually programmed into still lower species on the evolutionary ladder like ants and bees. (Cox, 2015). Do-gooding is essential for long-term survival of the species.

After this preliminary discussion let us revert to our question: What has gone wrong?

The very mindset!

Denial of a positive, independent, objectively existing value system, and ethics! The misplaced and misconceived aspiration that *I can become superman – ubermensch, and can frame my own ethics*, and its natural logical corollary that *others are sub-human*! The thought detaches the person affected with it from the rest of the species of *Homo sapiens*, and he or she stops thinking in terms of survival of the species, harbouring the thought that he or she was the *fittest* and will thus survive at the cost of annihilation of others, that he or she will become his or her own God one day.

Alas! My friend, whether you believe in the existence of God or not, you must be aware that the universe is too big and too complex for anyone as small as me or you to aspire to become God!

So, the basic malaise has its roots in any thought process supporting the super – man ideology in any form and what follows from it logically, the objective of wealth maximisation, seeing the globe as a market and not as a home or family, with a *good business sense and not a sense of do-gooding.*

What to do?

There is just one fundamental solution which can save the species *Homo sapiens* in its original natural habitat – the planet earth. Radical, as it might be there is no other solution. Or let me say that no other solution is going to work till we successfully and completely implement this one.

Reverse the thought process, as soon as possible!

Remember the following as an article of faith:

1. The globe is the sacred and sacrosanct home of the family of *Homo sapiens*. It cannot be looked upon as a market. Markets do exist within it. It does not exist within a market. Want to be patriotic? Love this home.

2. In a family, we have old parents incapable of earning, or our babies totally dependent on us or an ailing beloved or spouse who cannot be left to die. We have to care for them for a long-term survival of the species, with a sense of what you may like to call do-gooding and not with a good business sense.

3. Redefine good business sense, too. It cannot be wealth maximisation of shareholders. It has to be the maximisation of survival chance of *Homo sapiens*.

4. Do do-gooding, do do-gooding, do do-gooding – repeat this *mantra* 1000 times in the morning when you wake up and 1000 times when you go to bed, maybe on a rosary if you do not abhor one!

Before you close the book, let me try to answer another question.

What if people do not follow my advice?

No definite answer can be given but still who can stop us from fantasising or to take a mental dive into the fathomless future, may be like a sci-fi novelist.

There are two and only two possibilities. Either God exists or God does not exist. We are miserably incapable of conclusively deciding which one of the two possibilities is true. We cannot even assign a reliable probability estimate to the two possibilities.

Now supposing God exists. In that case prophesies in the scriptures which resemble so much in their broad content across different religions may come true. The most figurative are those in the Book of Revelation in the New Testament. Please go through it. For you, I quote only verse 18:14 through 18:18.

18:14And the fruits which thy soul lusted after are gone from thee, and all things that were dainty and sumptuous are perished from thee, and men shall find them no more at all. 18:15The merchants of these things, who were made rich, by her, shall stand afar off for the fear of her torment, weeping and mourning; 18:16saying Woe, woe, the great city, she that was arrayed in fine linen and purple and scarlet, and decked with gold and precious stone and pearl! 18:17for in an hour so great riches is made desolate. And every shipmaster, and every one that saileth any wither, and mariners and as many as gain their living by sea, stood afar off, 18:18and cried out as they looked upon the smoke of her burning, saying, what city is like the great city? (John)

If this is true, wealth maximisation, plunder of the resources of earth and worship of the goddess of wealth – fornication with the whore of Babylon, will attract a wrath from God and the plunderers and wealth maximisers will be doomed and destroyed and humanity will be saved through a *supreme intervention.*

If this is not true, and is only a superstition, then either the humanity shall, on its own, decide to shun the objective of wealth maximisation in favour of the objective of maximisation of survival chances of the species with a strong sense of do-gooding, or will continue looking at the globe as a market with a good business sense – read wealth maximisation – not a sense of do-gooding.

If the latter course is chosen, the apex of the pyramid will become leaner and sharper, with passing time as more and more wealth will be sucked to the top. The 1% of the population who control 50% of the wealth today will be controlling 51, 52, and 53 – may be 80% or even more of the wealth with the passage of time, through the working of a giant centrifugal wealth sucker pump. Wealth breeds innovation – both engineering and technological like space travel and financial like paper money and derivatives – and innovation in its turn, sucks more wealth from the bottom to the top. It is the working of this pump which explains the strange behaviour of money to flow against the gradient – a process which I have earlier called a process of reverse osmosis.

One day the natural resources on earth will be so badly exploited that it will be hard to breathe here. Meanwhile, extraterrestrial inhabitable worlds will be discovered. The 1% top or a smaller fraction of it will fly off to those worlds and settle there. This will create the necessary isolation and breeding barrier for organic evolution to take place. The genetic endowments of the two races will eventually get stabilised and two new species will be formed, the sub-humans – lower in rank and status than the present day *Homo sapiens* – because they will be left on a planet completely ruined and robbed of its resources, and the super humans or *ubermensch* the spacers who will fly off to other worlds taking away with them almost all the resources available on earth; much like the colonial rulers going away from the colonies.

I will suggest that the species of sub-humans left back down here may be called *Homo gaius*. I have derived the specific name *gaius*, derived from Gaia the personification of mother earth in Greek mythology. They will be an endangered species, will have extremely poor chances of survival, with a very high mortality rate, and sooner or later will become an extinct species.

I will like to call the other species, those who fly off to extraterrestrial habitats – the super humans, the *ubermensch* – as *Homo machiavellius*. I suggest the specific name *machiavellius*, in *'honour'* of Niccolo Machiavelli. In *'honour'* of him, because *the term Machiavellian is often associated with deceit, deviousness, ambition and brutality* (Wikipedia the free encyclopedia). Machiavellianism is a personality trait measured by psychologists on a scale called Mach scale. Persons high on Mach believe that *ends justify the means* and *I will do what it takes*. People high on Mach are more successful business managers than those who score low on the scale. I am not aware how much the trait is governed genetically, but, I suppose there might be some locus or a set of loci on the human DNA which code for this trait, capable of being selected, or otherwise, in the process of organic evolution. I think that people in the 1% population having 50% wealth of the globe are high on Mach. And if my fantasy (nightmare?) about speciation of *Homo sapiens* into *Homo machiavellius* and *Homo gaius* ever comes true, those leaving the planet to become the progenitors of *Homo machiavellius* will be highest on Mach!

Coming back to the present time when we are still one single species of *Homo sapiens*, if you belong to the 1% population at the pinnacle and if you are dead sure that there is no God or even if there is God, he will never intervene directly in the affairs of humans, and that the scriptures are nothing but superstitious tales, and you will be able to find a place in the outer space to go to and a means for a safe journey *before* earth gets destroyed irrecoverably, please go on maximising your wealth with a good business sense not a sense of do-gooding.

But if like me, you belong to the remaining 99% of world population, whether you believe in God or not or are still indecisive in this regard; then, remember, for your survival and for the survival of your progeny, you must start do-gooding yourself, try to convince more and more and more people that do-gooding is urgently needed on a massive scale and try to ensure that the objective of business is redefined and changed from wealth maximisation of shareholders to survival chance maximisation of *Homo sapiens*.

This you must do with a *good survival sense or instinct* for survival of yourself and your progeny fearing a day of distressful wrath when the earth will no longer remain safe to live on!

Even if you do not want to do, do do-gooding!

Disturbed, sentimentally?

Oh! I am sorry!

But didn't I forewarn you at the outset in the preface itself?

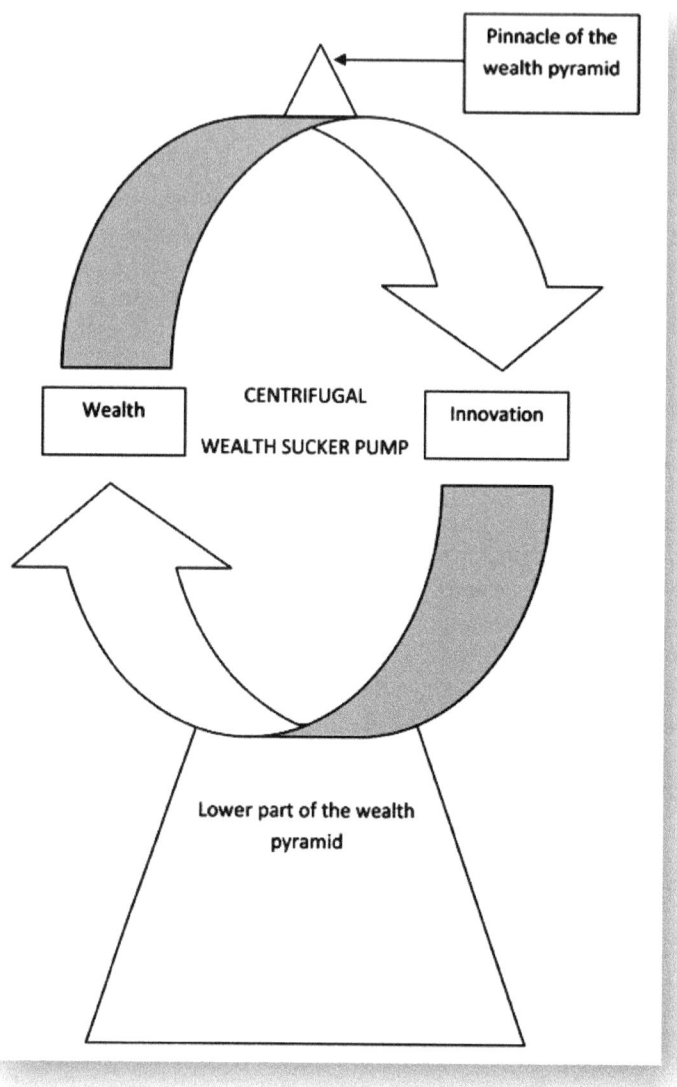

Illustration 4 Working of the centrifugal wealth sucker pump. (*Illustration: Masood Rezvi*)

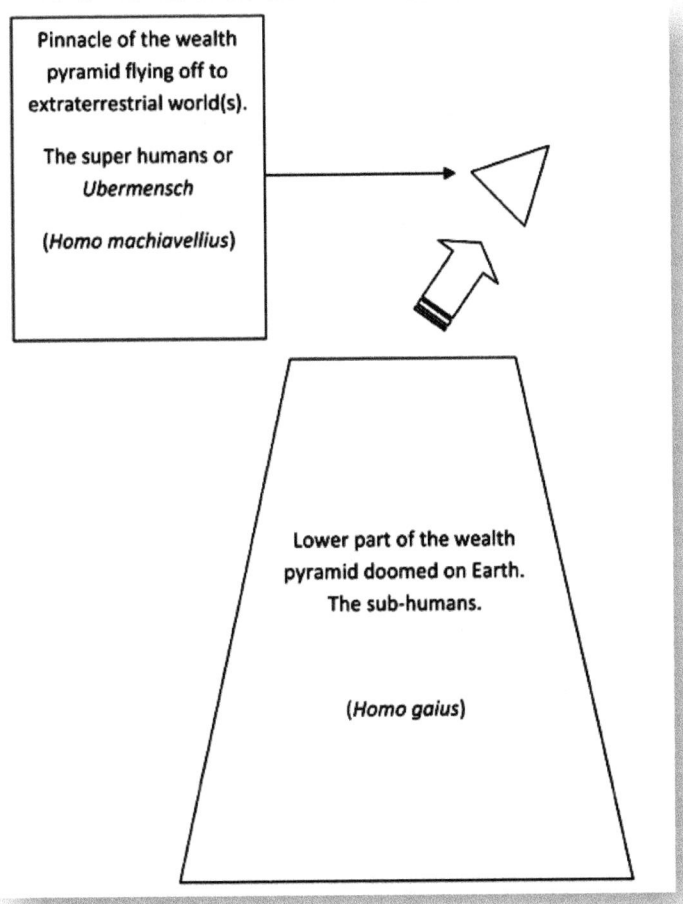

Illustration 5 Visualisation of possible speciation of
Homo sapiens into *Homo machiavellius* flying off to
extraterrestrial habitats in deep space and *Homo gaius*
the species of sub-humans to be doomed on planet
earth. (Illustration: Masood Rezvi)

76:8 And they feed food, for His love, (to) the indigent, the orphan, and the captive, 76:9 (saying) "We feed you for the sake of Allah (alone), no reward do we desire from you, nor thanks. 76:10 We only fear a Day of distressful Wrath from the side of our Lord."

(Al-Quran)

14 GLOSSARY

Agra   The famous city of Taj Mahal situated in the Uttar Pradesh state in India.

Aligarh   A town in the Uttar Pradesh state in India, which is famous for it Aligarh Muslim University, and for its lock industry.

Allah   The name, used in Al-Quran for the only creator, provider, and master of whatever exists. The Almighty.

Allahabad   A city in Uttar Pradesh state in India.

Allama   An erudite. The title used for a very highly learned scholar.

Amin   Field level recovery officials of the state government entrusted with the duty of collecting dues of land revenue from villagers.

Ayodhya   A town in Uttar Pradesh state in India which is revered by Hindus as the birthplace of the mythical prince and Hindu deity Rama.

B.Sc.   Bachelor of Science.

Babu   A term used to address a person in a clerical or assistant level function with respect.

Bengal	A province in pre-independence India consisting of West Bengal the present Indian state and Bangladesh.
Bhadohi	A town in the Uttar Pradesh state in India, famous for its carpet industry.
Bihar	An Indian state.
BIMARU	Acronym for Bihar (BI), Madhya Pradesh (MA), Rajasthan (R), and Uttar Pradesh (U), four Indian states with poor economic conditions.
Chhota Imambada	A mausoleum in Lucknow which is one of the main tourist attractions of the late medieval period.
Chit Fund	It is a kind of savings scheme run as per the Chit Funds Act, 1982.
CLERP 9	Corporate Law Economic Reform Program (Audit Reform & Corporate Disclosure) Act 2004, an Australian law.
Crore	10,000,000.
CSR	Corporate Social Responsibility.
Cuttack	A city in the Odisha state in India.
Dadri	A village in Ghaziabad district of Uttar Pradesh state in India around 50 KMs away from the national capital.
Dalits	Literally the downtrodden or the oppressed people. The term is now being used for those who in the caste system were traditionally treated as the lower caste in India. Other than the

upper three castes – the Brahmins (priests or scholars), the Kshatriyas (princes or warriors) and the Vaishyas (businessmen or traders).

Darbhanga   A town in the northern part of the Bihar states in India.

DGP   Director General Police.

Diwan   A collection of ghazals – a genre of Urdu poetry of any particular poet.

Diwani   Civil - civil administration and justice, as against faujdari - military.

DM   District Magistrate.

Dubagga   One of the casual labour markets in Lucknow where labourers flock every morning in the hope of being hired for the day by some construction agent or anyone requiring manual labour for a daily wage.

DWCRA   Development of Women and Children in Rural Area.

Etah   A town in the Uttar Pradesh state in India.

Etawah   A town in the Uttar Pradesh state in India.

Faizabad   A town in Uttar Pradesh state in India.

Firozabad   A town in the Uttar Pradesh state in India, famous for its glass work.

Gaia   The personification of Earth in Greek mythology.

GDP	Gross Domestic Product. A measure of economic production in the country.
Ghas Mandi	Literally grass market. A place in Lucknow where in olden days traders sold grass for horses. Now it is one of the casual labour markets where labourers flock every morning in the hope of being hired for the day by some construction agent or anyone requiring manual labour for a daily wage.
Ghaziabad	A city in Uttar Pradesh state in India adjacent to the national capital.
GoI	The government of India.
Gorakhpur	A city in the Uttar Pradesh state in India.
Gor-e-ghariban	Graveyard for the homeless poor.
G-Secs	Gilt-edged securities.
Hakeem	A practitioner of Unani medicine.
Hardoi	A town near Lucknow in the Uttar Pradesh state in India.
HIH	HIH Insurance was Australia's second largest insurance company.
Hyderabad	An Indian city. The capital of Andhra Pradesh state.
IRDP	Integrated Rural Development Programme.
Jharsuguda	A place in Odisha state in India.
Kabadiwallah	A trader dealing in the recyclable and

used material. A trash seller.

KM   Kilometre.

Kolkata   Calcutta. The Indian metropolis which is the capital of the state of West Bengal.

Lakh   100,000.

Lathicharge   Use of lathis – police cudgels to disperse a mob.

M.Sc.   Master of Science.

Maharajganj   A town in the Uttar Pradesh state in India.

Maharashtra   Indian state.

Mainpuri   A town in the Uttar Pradesh state in India.

Mumbi   The biggest metropolis, the business capital of India earlier called Bombay.

Muzaffarpur   A town in the northern part of the Bihar state in India.

Nani Amma   Mother's mother.

Netizens   Citizens of the Net. People who are active on the Internet.

NGO   Non-Governmental Organisation.

NHRC   National Human Rights Commission.

NIIT   National Institute of Information Technology.

Non-Performing   Irregular or delinquent loan accounts.

Assets

NPA	Non Performing Assets.
Orissa	Province in pre-independence India, now Odisha an Indian state.
Paise	One hundredth of a rupee.
Partawal	A village in Maharjganj district of the Uttar Pradesh state in India, which is a rice-growing belt.
Patna	The capital of Bihar state in India.
PC	Personal computer.
Pice	The old spelling of Paise, at that time a rupee consisted of sixteen Annas and each Anna of four Pice. Thus, each Rupee was divided in 64 Pice. Nowadays each Rupee has hundred Paise.
PMRY	Pradhan Mantri Rojgar Yojana (Prime Minister's Employment Scheme).
Ponzi	A fraudulent investment operation where the operator pays returns to its investors from new capital paid to the operator by new investors, rather than from profit earned by the operator.
PUCL	Public Union for Civil Liberties.
Pusa	A village in Samastipur district of north Bihar, where the first agricultural research station of the sub-continent the Imperial Agricultural Research Institute, was established and where now the Rajendra Agricultural University is situated.

Ranchi	The capital of the Jharkhand state in India.
Ratna	A jewel, a gem.
RBI	Reserve Bank of India, India's central bank.
RC	Recovery Certificate.
Ryot	The native Indian public in British India
Sa Re Ga Ma	Originally four Hindi alphabets used to denote the musical notes along with three more *Pa, Dha, Ni*. A musical contest organised by the Zee TV.
Samastipur	A town in the northern part of the Bihar state in India.
SC/ST	Scheduled Castes/Scheduled Tribes – Those identified castes and tribes which were traditionally treated and lowest in the traditional caste system and who have been scheduled by the GoI for positive action – the Dalits.
sci-fi	Science fiction.
SCP	Special Component Plan.
SEBI	Securities and Exchange Board of India.
SEEUY	Self Employment for Educated Unemployed Youth.
SEPUP	Self Employment Programme for Urban Poor.
SEUUP	Scheme for Economic Upliftment of

Urban Poor.

SLBC   State Level Bankers Committee.

SMS   Short Messaging Service on a phone.

Snow Job   A typical hardball technique used in distributive bargaining in which the negotiators overwhelm the other party with so much information that he or she has trouble which facts are real or important, and which are included as distractions. Governments use this technique frequently when releasing information publicly. (Lewicki, Saunders, & Barry, 2008).

Tehsildar   A magisterial level official in the state revenue department.

TOI   The Times of India.

U.P.   Uttar Pradesh state in India

Ubermensch   The superman – Friedrich Nietzsche's answer to the problem of Nihilism. Nietzsche begins his premise with the assumption that God does not exist, thus objective morality and inherent value are not possible since (according to his assumption) there is no ultimate being that exists to create morality and value in first place. Nietzsche's Ubermensch will act his own god, giving himself morality and values as he sees fit according to him alone. (urbandictionary.com).

Unani Medicine   Greek medicine, the system of cure practiced by pre-British – mainly Muslim – doctors.

UP	Uttar Pradesh state in India
Zamindar	In pre-independence India an aristocrat typically hereditary, who held enormous tracts of land and held control, from the zamindars, reserved the right to collect tax.
Zamindari	The system of tax collection through zamindars introduced by Cornwallis in India.
Zonal	Pertaining to a zone.
Zonal Office	Administrative office controlling and managing the affairs of regional offices and branches in that zone. Below the head office and above the regional offices in the zone, in the hierarchy in those days.

ABOUT THE AUTHOR

Masood joined Indian nationalised banking industry as an agriculture officer in 1983 and served in different positions, in different areas during his 17-year long career in banking. He has a rich experience of microfinance and recovery of bad debts in the banking industry, and wide exposure to the urban and rural poor in the largest Indian state of Uttar Pradesh.

In the Year 2000, he left his banking career as a manager from the zonal office of Punjab National Bank, tried his hands on entrepreneurship, photography and study of poor people's living conditions, study of financial management, and finally joined academics and is teaching finance, economics and accounting as a visiting faculty at Unity Degree College, Lucknow, India. He is actively involved in different philanthropic activities. He has attended many seminars and conferences and has published many papers and articles in various journals and newspapers.

He is a member of Indian Institute of Banking and Finance (IIBF), Mumbai and Commerce and Management Research Association (CAMRA), Lucknow.

Masood is the founder and managing trustee of Lucknow Educational and Development Trust (LEAD TRUST), Lucknow.

He was nominated, a member of the State Level Committee for Monitoring and Evaluation of Prime Minister's 15 Point Programme for Minorities by the Government of Uttar Pradesh.

Academically, he is M.Sc. Agriculture, MBA Finance, UGC-NET, and CAIIB(I). He was trained in Rural Development Projects at College of Agricultural Banking (CAB), Pune, India. He can be contacted through Facebook page for this book at https://m.facebook.com/povertynoose.